Collins

11+
Non-Verbal Reasoning

Complete Revision, Practice & Assessment

For GL Assessment

Introduction

The 11+ Non-Verbal Reasoning Test

In most cases, the 11+ selection tests are set by GL Assessment, CEM or the individual school. You should be able to find out which tests your child will be taking on the website of the school they are applying to or from the local authority.

It is particularly important to provide non-verbal reasoning practice as your child may not have come across these types of question before. Non-verbal reasoning assesses a child's ability to see patterns and relationships independent of language. The questions feature shapes, pictures and patterns and allow children to demonstrate their ability to analyse, deduce and infer from close observation.

Non-verbal reasoning tests provide schools with an indication of a child's potential to work successfully with abstract concepts and solve spatial reasoning problems. The results are good indicators of future learning and success in a number of subject areas.

About this Book

This book is split into three sections to help your child to prepare for the GL Assessment test in non-verbal reasoning. Features of each section include:

Revision
* Easy-to-digest revision notes for each topic.
* Develops the skills needed to answer test questions.
* 'Remember' boxes to emphasise key points and provide tips.
* Quick Tests to check understanding of a topic before moving on to the next.

Practice
* Topic-based questions to practise the necessary skills.
* Increases familiarity with the questions expected in the test.
* Tests are timed to develop the ability to work at speed.

Assessment
* Four practice papers offer multiple opportunities to have a go at a test and gradually improve performance.
* Familiarises your child with the format of the papers.
* Enables your child to practise working at speed and with accuracy.

Answers and explanations are provided at the back of the book to help you mark your child's answers and support their preparation.

Progress charts are also included to help you record scores on the practice tests and practice papers.

ebook

To access the ebook visit collins.co.uk/ebooks and follow the step-by-step instructions.

2   11+ Non-Verbal Reasoning

The Practice Papers

Spend some time talking with your child, so that they understand the purpose of the practice papers and how doing them will help them to prepare for the actual exam.

Agree with your child a good time to take the practice papers. This should be when they are fresh and alert. You also need to find a good place to work, a place that is comfortable and free from distractions. Being able to see a clock is helpful as they learn how to pace themselves.

Explain how they may find some parts easy and others more challenging, but that they need to have a go at every question. If they 'get stuck' on a question, they should just mark it with an asterisk and carry on. At the end of the paper, they may have time to go back and try again.

Multiple-choice tests
For this style of test, the answers are recorded on a separate answer sheet and not in the question booklet. This answer sheet will often be marked by a computer for the actual exam, so it is important that it is used correctly.

Answers should be indicated by drawing a clear pencil line through the appropriate box and there should be no other marks. If your child indicates one answer and then wants to change their response, the first mark must be fully rubbed out. Practising with an answer sheet now will reduce the chance of your child getting anxious or confused during the actual test.

Answer sheets for the practice papers can be found at the very back of the book on pages 153–160. Further copies can be downloaded from **collins.co.uk/11plus**.

How much time should be given?
In this book, each practice paper is made up of five sections, with instructions, an example and some practice questions at the beginning of each section, followed by 12 questions. In the actual exam, each section would be administered and timed separately, with the invigilator reading out the instructions, checking the practice questions and then timing the section. For the purposes of practising, however, the papers can be used in different ways, and two options are set out below.

1. Read through the instructions with your child. Get them to complete the practice questions and check the answer key, then allow six minutes for the 12 test questions. If they have not finished in the time, ask them to mark the question they are on and then complete the section. When marking the test, you will be able to see how many questions would have been answered correctly in the time available. Repeat for the other four sections. This option is closest to the real exam.

2. Simply give the practice paper to your child and get them to read the instructions and work through the paper by themselves without any help or guidance. They should work through the questions with a clock/watch/timer to help them practise working within the allowed time.

Marking
Award one mark for each correct answer. Half marks are not allowed. No marks are deducted for wrong answers.

Note: The practice test papers are designed to reflect the style of GL Assessment tests, but the score achieved on these papers is no guarantee that your child will achieve a score of the same standard on the formal tests. Other factors, such as the standard of responses from all candidates, will determine their success in the formal exam.

Acknowledgements

The authors and publisher are grateful to the copyright holders for permission to use quoted materials and images.

All images are © HarperCollins*Publishers* Ltd

Every effort has been made to trace copyright holders and obtain their permission for the use of copyright material. The authors and publisher will gladly receive information enabling them to rectify any error or omission in subsequent editions. All facts are correct at time of going to press.

Published by Collins

An imprint of HarperCollins*Publishers*

1 London Bridge Street

London SE1 9GF

HarperCollins*Publishers*

Macken House, 39/40 Mayor Street Upper,

Dublin 1, D01 C9W8, Ireland

ISBN: 978-0-00-839887-3

First published 2020

10 9 8 7 6 5 4 3

British Library Cataloguing in Publication Data.

A CIP record of this book is available from the British Library.

Publishers: Clare Souza and Katie Sergeant

Contributing authors: Neil R Williams, Peter Francis, Beatrix Woodhead and Pamela Macey

Project Development and Management: Richard Toms and Rebecca Skinner

Reviewer: Maravandio Ltd (trading as The Sensible Tuition Company)

Cover Design: Kevin Robbins and Sarah Duxbury

Inside Concept Design and Page Layout: Ian Wrigley

Production: Karen Nulty

Printed in the United Kingdom

This book contains FSC™ certified paper and other controlled sources to ensure responsible forest management.

For more information visit: www.harpercollins.co.uk/green

Contents

Revision

Practice

Assessment

Answers

Question Types and Strategies

You should be able to:

- identify the type of question you have been given
- use appropriate methods to tackle each type of question
- follow instructions to give your answer correctly and clearly.

Non-Verbal Reasoning Tests

- Non-verbal reasoning tests are usually broken up into five or six sections.
- Each section will have questions of just one type in it. This makes the test a little easier as you can get into a rhythm for each section much more readily.

Most Unlike

- When you are working with 'most unlike' questions, you simply need to look at the images and decide which one of them doesn't quite fit with the rest. In other words, you are finding which image is the odd one out.

Example
Look at these five images. Work out what connects four of the images and makes the other image **most unlike** the others.

A   B   C   D   E

- Each shape is made from eight segments, four on the outside and four on the inside:
    - The first shape has alternating black and white segments.
    - The second has an even number of spotted and white segments.
    - The third has white, spotted and black segments.
    - The fourth has an even number of black and white segments.
    - The fifth shape has alternating white and spotted segments.
- The next step is to find the odd one out:
    - Shape **C** seems to stand out as all of the outer segments are white and there are two different types of shading on the inner segments.
    - All four of the other shapes have half of their segments in white and half as either spotted or black. Half of the outer segments are white, and half of the inner segments are white.
- Shape **C** is most unlike because the other shapes have two outer segments in white and two inner segments in white, but **C** does not.

Remember

The questions are multiple choice so have a go at every question. You will need to work quickly so make an educated guess where you are not quite sure of the answer.

Most Like

- 'Most like' questions can be some of the most difficult to answer as you have to decide which connection is the most important.
- In these questions you could be shown two or three images on the left that are related by at least one connection. You then have to pick one image to join that group.

> **Example**
> Work out what makes the three images on the left similar to each other. Then find the image on the right that is **most like** the three images on the left.
>
>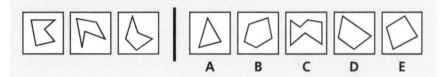

- In this example, the three images on the left all look like random shapes. However, when you look closely they do have some similarities:
  - The first shape has five sides, four acute angles and one reflex angle.
  - The second shape has five sides, three acute angles, one obtuse angle and one reflex angle.
  - The third shape has five sides, two acute angles, two obtuse angles and one reflex angle.
- The **two** connections are that the shapes all have five sides and one reflex angle. It is possible that only one connection is relevant and that the other is a distraction.
- Describing the features of each possible answer in the same way helps you to work out which option is correct:
  - Shape **A** has three sides and no reflex angles.
  - Shape **B** has five sides and no reflex angles.
  - Shape **C** has seven sides and two reflex angles.
  - Shape **D** has four sides and no reflex angles.
  - Shape **E** has four sides and no reflex angles.
- None of the options has a single reflex angle so it looks like that is a distraction.
- The connection you are looking for is a shape with five sides. Only shape **B** has five sides, so that is the correct answer.

> **Remember**
>
> An acute angle is less than 90°.
>
> An obtuse angle is between 90° and 180°.
>
> A reflex angle is greater than 180°.

Grid Questions

- While a lot of the questions you see use boxes, grid questions take this one step further and put the boxes together to make either 2 × 2 or 3 × 3 grids.
- Within the grid one box will be empty and you have to pick the box that should fill it from the multiple-choice options given.

- These questions can use a wide range of connections. They commonly use reflections, which are easy to see in the grid as the grid lines give you the mirror line. More complex problems have two or three changes happening between the boxes, often with a number of shapes within each box.
- Look at the following example and see if you can work out which of the possible answers completes the grid. The fully worked answer is on page 30.

Example
One of the boxes is missing from the grid on the left. Work out which of the five boxes on the right completes the grid.

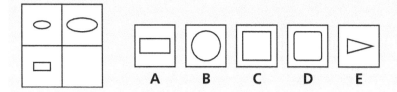

Repeat the Changes

- The skill in 'repeat the changes' questions is to work out the connection between the first two shapes before applying this to the third shape.

Example
Work out how the first pair of images go together. Then find the image that completes the second pair in the same way as the first pair.

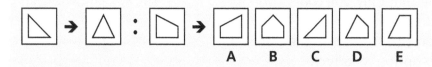

- Notice that:
  - the first shape on the left is a right-angled triangle
  - the second shape is an equilateral triangle
  - both triangles have the same length base, which is parallel to the bottom of the box.
- Think about the difference between the shapes: the top point of the triangle has moved to the middle of the box.
- Now look at the third box, to see what sort of shape you have been asked to work with: the third shape is an irregular quadrilateral.
- Consider what the shape will look like if the same change is applied: it will remain an irregular quadrilateral with the same length base parallel to the bottom of the box, but the top point will move to the middle of the box.
- Shape **D** is the correct answer.

Breaking Codes

- 'Breaking codes' is a unique question type that often appears in non-verbal reasoning tests. The reason it is unique is that it uses letters for the codes you need to break; no other question type has letter codes within the questions.
- You could be given five images like those shown in the example below:
  - Every image will have a code either underneath it or beside it. Those codes will contain one, two or three letters.
  - Each letter in the code represents a different feature within the image. As that feature changes, so will the letter. The first letter of each image will link to one feature, the second to another, and so on.
- All you need to do is break the code and work out what all the letters mean so that you can pick the right code from the options you are given.
- Try to work out the answer code for the example below. The example is fully worked through on page 18.

Example

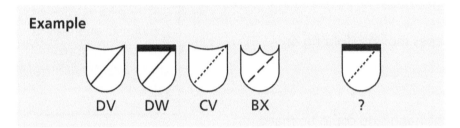

Complete the Sequence

- Another common question type is 'complete the sequence'. In these questions you are usually shown five boxes. Four of them have an image and one of them is empty. The empty box can be anywhere within the sequence.
- It is easier if it is the first or the last box that is empty as you will have four images in a row to work out the pattern from. The harder questions often have the middle box as the empty one.

Example

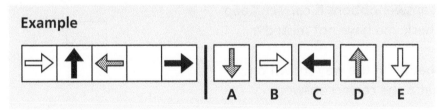

- The first thing to do is to work out what is changing as you go from one box to the next:
  - The arrow is rotating 90° anti-clockwise.
  - The shading changes from white to black to spotted to **something** to black.
- The shading change sounds like a big clue, but you need to ask what that missing something could be:

- The second and fifth boxes have black arrows, so there is a good chance that the shading in the first box should match the shading in the fourth box. This means the arrow in there should be white.
  - If the arrow is going anti-clockwise, it should end up pointing down in the fourth box.
- Putting the clues together, you want a white arrow that is pointing down. The correct answer is option **E**.

Spatial Reasoning

- Spatial reasoning tests your ability to imagine how 2D and 3D shapes would look if they were rotated or altered in some way.
- Spatial reasoning questions can come in several different forms, including:
  - nets and cubes
  - paper folding and hole punching
  - 3D shape rotations
  - find the hidden shape
  - make a shape
  - plans and elevations.
- You may need to imagine the shapes moving, folding or altering in some way.

Remember

The best way to practise spatial reasoning is to check how shapes change using 3D objects. Experiment folding pieces of paper or building structures from toy blocks and seeing how they look from above and from different sides.

Example
Which of the shapes on the right-hand side could be made from all of the figures on the left?

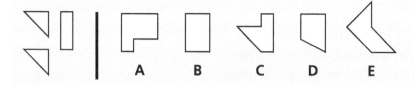

- The first thing to do is to imagine the shapes on the left-hand side being pushed together. Work methodically and imagine the figures being overlaid on top of each answer option in turn.
- Even if you think one of the first answer options is correct, keep testing all the other options to check you have not missed a better answer.
- Here the figures could be put together in the way shown on the right to form option **A**, so that is the correct answer.

Making Connections

You should be able to:

- identify the common connection types and identify the image that doesn't share a connection in a group of regular or irregular shapes
- identify the similarities and differences between shapes
- identify and discard the distractions.

Recognising the Most Common Connection Types

- A connection is something that two or more images have in common such as the number of corners, the shading, the pattern of lines, the shape or size.
- Sometimes you will see two common connections and you will need to decide which is the most important connection. Most common connection questions ask you to find one image that doesn't share a connection with the others; the 'odd one out'.

Identifying the 'Odd One Out' in a Group of Regular Shapes

Example

Look at the five images. Work out what connects four of the images and makes the other image **most unlike** the others.

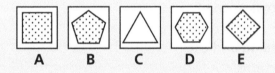

A   B   C   D   E

- Look at the five shapes in the example:
  - All of the shapes have straight lines.
  - All of the shapes are regular.
  - All of the shapes have solid outlines.
  - Four of the images have the same pattern.
- There is also one less obvious connection in these shapes. Look carefully at the number of sides:
  - Three of the images have an even number of sides.
  - Two of the images have an odd number of sides.
- You can ignore the first three connections above as they link all of the images together, making it impossible to pick an odd one out. You can also ignore the final connection as no single image is different.
- The shading pattern is therefore the important connection. The correct answer is option **C** as it is most unlike the others.

> **Remember**
>
> Regular shapes are shapes where all the sides are the same length and the angles are the same size.
>
> Squares and equilateral triangles are both regular shapes.
>
>

Identifying the 'Odd One Out' in a Group of Irregular Shapes

Example
Look at these five images. Work out what connects four of the images and makes the other image **most unlike** the others.

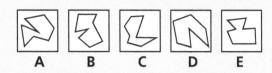

A   B   C   D   E

- In this set of shapes, there are no shading patterns to consider:
  - All of the shapes are made up of straight lines.
  - All of the lines are solid.
  - None of the shapes are regular.
- These connections do not help as they refer to all of the shapes, so you need to look at each shape in more detail.
- With questions involving irregular shapes, it is often a good idea to count the number of sides or types of angles in each shape. This also applies when there is more than one shape in each box; these can be regular or irregular.
- All the shapes have eight sides apart from **D**, which has seven. The correct answer is therefore **D**.

> **Remember**
>
> There are a wide range of shading patterns that can be used in non-verbal reasoning questions; some have lines, some have blocked patterns and some have spots. There can also be subtle variations with vertical, horizontal and diagonal lines counting as different patterns. The lines around the images may also have different patterns such as dots or dashes.

Identifying Connections Involving Direction

- Questions involving direction will often use arrows as they clearly point in a particular way.
- Along with the direction, the style of the arrowhead and the number of fins on the tail can be used as connections.

Example
Look at the two images on the left. Decide what makes these two images similar to each other. Now find the image on the right that is **most like** the two images on the left.

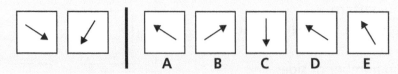

A   B   C   D   E

- Look closely at the two images on the left and work out what the connection between their directions might be:
  - The first arrow is pointing down and to the right.
  - The second arrow is pointing down and to the left.
  - Both arrows are pointing downwards.
- Only having two images to work with can make it easy to find a general direction, but remember that sometimes you will

be given three images to compare. Now check the possible answers to see which ones are pointing downwards:
- Options **A**, **B**, **D** and **E** are pointing upwards.
- Option **C** is pointing downwards.
- The correct answer is option **C**. It is most like the two images on the left.

Identifying Connections Involving Angles

- When two lines connect, you get an angle. Angles can be acute, obtuse, reflex or right angles.
- Where angles are the connection, you will be looking for the same number of angles of a certain type within all of the images.

> **Example**
> Look at the three images on the left. Decide what makes these three images similar to each other. Now find the image on the right that is **most like** the three images on the left.
>
>
>   **A**   **B**   **C**   **D**   **E**

- Look at the angles in the three shapes on the left to see if there is a connection:
  - The first shape has three acute angles.
  - The second shape has three acute angles.
  - The third shape has three acute angles.
- All of the shapes have three acute angles so this is the connection.
- Have a look at the five possible answers to see what sorts of angle they have:
  - Option **A** has three acute angles.
  - Options **B**, **D** and **E** have a right angle.
  - Option **C** has an obtuse angle.
- There is only one option that could match – option **A** is the correct answer.

Identifying Connections Involving Symmetry

- In non-verbal reasoning questions you should think of symmetry as being within an image and reflection being a reflection of a whole image.
- Symmetry within images is one of the least common connections. This is because finding shapes with an equal number of lines of symmetry can be difficult.
- There are two lines of symmetry that may be used in these questions: a **vertical** line of symmetry where everything on the

left is matched to what is on the right, and a **horizontal** line of symmetry where everything at the top is matched to the bottom.

Example

Look at the three images on the left. Decide what makes these three images similar to each other. Now find the image on the right that is **most like** the three images on the left.

   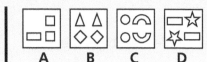

A   B   C   D   E

- Have a look at the three images and decide which sort of symmetry each one has:
  - The first image has a horizontal line of symmetry.
  - The second image has a horizontal line of symmetry and a vertical line of symmetry.
  - The third image has a horizontal line of symmetry.
- All of the images have horizontal lines of symmetry so this is your connection.
- Have a look at the five possible answers to see if they have any lines of symmetry:
  - Option **A** has no lines of symmetry.
  - Option **B** has a vertical line of symmetry.
  - Option **C** has a horizontal line of symmetry.
  - Option **D** has no lines of symmetry.
  - Option **E** has no lines of symmetry.
- There is only one option that could match – option **C** is the correct answer.

Remember

Watch out for triangles and stars when looking for symmetry within an image. These shapes are easily missed but can give a clue to the direction of symmetry.

Identifying Similarities and Differences Between Single Shapes

- The simplest comparison you will have to make is between individual shapes.
- You should consider: the shape itself; the number of sides or corners; the line and shading styles; the angles.

Example

Look at the five images. Work out what connects **four** of the images and makes the other image the odd one out.

A   B   C   D   E

- Look closely at the five images and see how many similarities you can find:
  - All the images are of triangles.
  - All the images are shaded white.
- Now look at the images again and see how many differences you can find:
  - Triangles **A**, **C**, **D** and **E** are equilateral triangles. Triangle **B** is a right-angled triangle.
  - Triangles **A** and **D** have solid sides while triangles **B**, **C** and **E** have dashed sides.
- The odd one out is **B** as this is the only triangle with a right angle; the line style is a distraction.

Identifying Similarities and Differences Between Groups of Shapes

- Three of the most common similarities are:
  - the number of sides or corners
  - the number of items in each box
  - lines of symmetry.
- Look closely at the two images shown right and see how many **similarities** you can find:
  - All of the shapes have solid sides.
  - All of the shapes are shaded white.
  - Each image has a total of 12 sides and 12 corners.
- Now look at the two images again and see how many **differences** you can find:
  - The first image has three shapes, but the second has four shapes.
  - The first image has three different shapes, but the second has four identical triangles.
  - The second image has four lines of symmetry, but the first has none.

Identifying Similarities and Differences Between Segmented Shapes

- More complicated questions often involve segmented shapes as there are more elements to compare when looking for similarities and differences.
- Look closely at the two images shown right and see how many similarities you can find:
  - Both are squares split into eight triangular segments.
  - Both have black, white and spotted segments.
  - All of the lines are solid.
  - Both images have three black segments.

Spotting Distractions

- Some questions give you more information than you need. These extra pieces of information are distractions and being able to discard them is an important skill.

> **Example**
> Look at the three images on the left. Decide what makes these three images similar to each other. Now find the image on the right that is **most like** the three images on the left.
>
>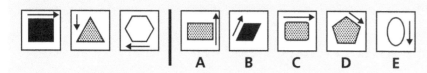
>
> A   B   C   D   E

- Look closely at the three images on the left and see how many connections you can find:
  - All three boxes contain a simple arrow, but they are all pointing in different directions.
  - All three boxes contain a regular shape, but they all have different types of shading.
- When you have connections that seem to be confusing, look at the possible answers to see whether or not they give any clues:
  - All of the options have a simple arrow, but they are also pointing in different directions. This suggests it is a distraction – there to catch your eye and confuse you, but not relevant. Imagine the arrows are not there.
  - The options all have one shape with varying shading patterns. The one shape might be relevant but the different shading patterns are not. Imagine all the shapes on the left are shaded black:

- Removing the distractions makes the question much easier. Have a look at the question again, ignoring the distractions, and see what you can now find. The three images are all regular shapes.
- Looking at the options, only one is a regular shape and that is image **D**.

Quick Test

1. Look at the five shapes in each row. What connects **four** of the shapes and makes the other shape the odd one out? Find the shape that is **most unlike** the others.

a)

   A   B   C   D   E

b)

   A   B   C   D   E

2. The two shapes on the left are part of a set. Which of the five shapes on the right belongs with the set?

a)
  |

               A   B   C   D   E

b)
 |

               A   B   C   D   E

3. The two images on the left are part of a set. Which of the five images on the right belongs with the set?

a)
  |

               A   B   C   D   E

b)
  |

               A   B   C   D   E

4. The two boxes on the left are part of a set. Which of the five boxes on the right belongs with the set?

  |

               A   B   C   D   E

Breaking Codes

You should be able to:

- identify common letters and the features they represent
- work out the remaining code by matching up the remaining features.

Codes with Two Letters

- Codes with two letters often represent images that have only two features that change, so the task is to link one of the letters with one of the two features. You will then know that the second letter refers to the remaining feature.

   Example
   The four images on the left each have a code. Work out how the codes go with these images. Now find the correct code from the list on the right that matches the fifth image.

Identifying a Common Feature

- Look at the letters before looking at the images. Identifying common letters will tell you which images to compare to begin working out the code.
- The first two shields share the same first letter, D. This tells you that they will have an identical feature.

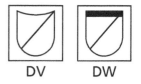

- Now look at the images and try to identify the features within them:
  - DV is a shield with a curved top and a solid black line going across it diagonally.
  - DW is a shield with a straight top and a solid black line going across it diagonally.
- Once you have identified the common features you will need to check the other images and codes to see if these features match any other images.

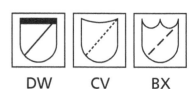

- In this case there are no identical lines or other codes with a D.
- D represents the solid black line going across the shield diagonally.
- Knowing one code often provides a shortcut to working out some remaining codes. Here we know the first letter relates to the diagonal line across the shield:
  - D is a solid line.
  - C is a dotted line.
  - B is a dashed line.

Working Out the Remaining Code

- By working out the first letter of each code, it is easier to decipher the second as you have already eliminated one feature (the diagonal line in this case).
- Look for other features in the images that you haven't linked to a code. In this example, the only other changing feature is the shape of the shield. Begin with the first letter in the question – V:
  - DV is a shield with a curved top.
  - CV is a shield with a curved top as well so this must be the code for V.
- You now need to examine the shield shape linked to the remaining two code letters to work out what they represent:
  - V has a single curve at the top.
  - W has a thick black line at the top.
  - X has two curves at the top.
- Working out the code for each feature means that you can confidently work out the missing code for the final shield.
- Try working out the code without looking at the options and then check to make sure the option has been provided in the answers.
- The image is a shield with a dotted line going diagonally across it and a thick black line at the top. Therefore you should end up with the code CW for the fifth image.
- Answer the question as you have been instructed and mark the option **C**.

?

Solving Problems With More Than Two Features

- When more than two features are present in codes with two letters, the questions are slightly more difficult to answer but the method is the same. You just have to work methodically to identify what each letter represents.

> **Example**
> The four images on the left each have a code. Work out how the codes go with these images. Now find the correct code from the list on the right that matches the fifth image.
>
>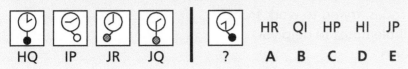
>
> | HR | QI | HP | HI | JP |
> |----|----|----|----|----|
> | A | B | C | D | E |

Identifying a Feature with Common Letters

- Don't be distracted by the more complex images in these questions; begin by looking at the code letters as you did before.
- First find a pair of common letters and identify the features:
  - The letter J is common to the third and fourth shapes.
  - JR is a clock with a spotted pendulum that has swung to the left. The time is about eight o'clock.

- JQ is a clock with a spotted pendulum that is in the middle of its swing. The time is about half-past two.
- When you have identified the common feature, you can ignore the others and work out the rest of the code:
  - H is a black pendulum.
  - I is a white pendulum.
  - J is a spotted pendulum.

Cracking Codes by Letter Position

- You now know that the first letter is linked to the colour of the pendulum, so you can discount this feature when moving on to the second letter.
- If there are more than two features, as there are in this example, continue to work in the same way as you did before, looking at each of the remaining features.

Finding the Second Feature

- Look for another pair of letters and identify the common features:
  - The first and fourth images both have Q in their codes.
  - HQ is a clock with a black pendulum that is in the middle of its swing. The time is about two o'clock.
  - JQ is a clock with a spotted pendulum that is in the middle of its swing. The time is about half-past two.
- When you have identified the common feature, you can ignore the others and work out the rest of the code.
- All the images are clocks, so the second letter must represent the position of the pendulum, but not the shading of it.
- Check the position of the pendulum in relation to each letter:
  - P is a pendulum that has swung to the right.
  - Q is a pendulum in the middle of its swing.
  - R is a pendulum that has swung to the left.
- Now you have worked out the code you can answer the question. The code for the fifth image is HP (option **C**).

> **Remember**
>
> Code questions often contain distractions to confuse you. Both the clock faces and the times in this example were distractions and included to confuse you.

Codes with Three Letters

- Codes with three letters represent images with three features that change, so the task is to link the letters with one of the three features.
- Work methodically to identify the codes, trying to work from left to right if you can. You can scribble notes to help you remember what each letter represents.

Example

The four images on the left each have a code. Work out how the codes go with these images. Now find the code from the list on the right that matches the fifth image.

       SJX SKY TKW RSW TJW

| RJW | SKW | RKY | TJX | | ? | A | B | C | D | E |

Identifying Common Letters in Codes

- As with two-letter codes, before looking at the images you should first focus on the letters. Common letters will tell you which images to compare. Try to find two codes that only share the first letter.
- In the example, the codes for the first and third images both begin with the letter R. This tells you there is going to be something identical about them.
- Now look at the images and try to identify the features within them:
  - RJW has white and spotted segments on the outside with white and striped segments in the middle. The segments are in line with each other.
  - RKY has white and spotted segments on the outside with white and black segments on the inside. The segments do not line up.
- It looks like R represents the white and spotted segments around the outer circle. Now you need to check the other images and codes to see if the feature and the letter match any other images.
- In this case there are no other images with white and spotted outer segments or other codes with an R, so this must be the correct answer to the code.
- As the first letter of the code must stand for a related feature, you can now work out the codes for the remaining first letters. In the code above, the first letter represents the shading in the outer segments:
  - R is for white and spotted.
  - S is for white and black.
  - T is for white and striped.

Deciphering the Second Code Letter

- Now move on to the second letter in the code and work out which feature it represents.
- Look for other features in the images that you haven't linked to a code. There are two features that are changing – the shading of the inner segments and whether or not the segments are in line with each other.
- As you know what the first letter represents you can ignore it for now:
  - SKW has white and striped inner segments which are not in line with the outer segments.
  - RKY has white and black inner segments which are not in line with the outer segments.
- The common feature is that the segments are not in line with each other.
- You now need to examine the images to work out the letters for the middle of the code:
  - J shows the segments are in line with each other.
  - K shows the segments are not in line with each other.

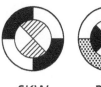

SKW   RKY

Working Out the Remaining Codes

- Finally you are ready to tackle the third code letter, and at this stage there should be only one possible feature left.
- Look for two images that share their final code letter. In this case there are two that share the letter W. As you know the features for the first two letters, you can ignore them:
  - RJW has white and striped inner segments.
  - SKW has white and striped inner segments.

RJW   SKW

- Therefore white and striped inner segments are represented by the letter W.
- You now need to examine the images linked to the remaining two code letters to complete the code:
  - W is for white and striped inner segments.
  - Y is for white and black inner segments.
  - X is for white and spotted inner segments.
- Working out the code for each letter means that you can confidently work out the missing code for the final image.
- Try working out the code without looking at the options and then check to make sure the option has been provided in the answers.
- The image has white and striped segments on both the inside and outside, and the segments are in line with each other. The code for those features is TJW.
- Answer the question as you have been instructed. In this case you should mark the answer **E**.

?

Quick Test

1. The four boxes on the left each have a code. Work out how the codes go with these boxes. Now find the correct code from the list on the right that matches the fifth box.

AM   CL   BM   CN   ?

AL CM BN AN BL

  A   B   C   D   E

2. The four shapes on the left each have a code. Work out how the codes go with these shapes. Now find the correct code from the list on the right that matches the fifth shape.

EJX   DHY   DIZ   EJY   ?

DHZ EHX DJY EIX EHZ

  A   B   C   D   E

Finding Relationships

You should be able to:

- identify the relationship between shapes within an image and apply the relationship to shapes within another image
- match the proportions of one image to a different image
- identify how a shape has been moved within an image, find the links used to form larger shapes and apply the relationship to another image
- recognise and apply reflections and rotations.

Changing Shapes

- Changing shapes is all about spotting a range of connections. These connections together make a set of step-by-step instructions that you can apply to another image.
- The connections could be:
  - shading changes
  - shapes moving or even swapping places
  - the number of shapes
  - size changes and rotations.

Example

Look at the pair of images on the left connected by an arrow. Work out how the two images go together. Now look at the third image, which is followed by another arrow. Work out which of the five images on the right completes the second pair in the same way.

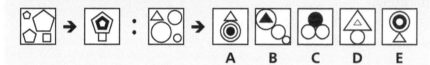

Finding the Connections

- Look closely at the first two images in the example. There are three changes that occur:
  - The three pentagons move to go one inside the other.
  - The medium-sized pentagon is then shaded black.
  - The small square is then moved underneath the pentagons.

Applying the Relationship to Another Image

- Once you have worked out the relationship, you have to apply it to a different set of shapes. Have a look at the third box. It has three circles and one triangle.
- You need to apply the relationship to the third box:
  - Move the three circles together to go one inside the other.
  - Shade the medium-sized circle black.
  - Move the triangle underneath the circles.

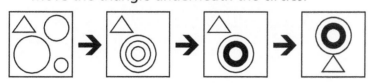

- Now compare this image with the possible answers. Option **E** is a perfect match and is the correct answer.

Proportion

- You may see segmented shapes with shading patterns. These questions will often include additional elements, such as rotation.

> **Example**
> Look at the two images on the left. Decide what makes these two images similar to each other.
>
> Now find the image on the right that is **most like** the two images on the left.
>
> |
>   **A**   **B**   **C**   **D**   **E**

Identifying a Pattern

- Look closely at the first two images in the example and see how the shaded areas are alike:
  - All of the shading is black.
  - Both images have two shaded segments on the outside.
  - Both images have two shaded segments on the inside.
  - The shaded segments on the inside are next to each other.

Identifying the Proportions in an Image

- Look at these first two images again and count how many segments there are of each type of shading.
- On shapes like these it is a good idea to treat the outer segments and inner segments separately:
  - There are eight outer segments in each image; two are black and the remaining six are white. The ratio of black to white is 1:3.
  - There are eight inner segments in each image; two are black and the remaining six are white. The ratio of black to white is 1:3.

Matching the Proportions to the Answer

- Have a look at the possible answers and see which ones fit each connection:
  - All of the options have black shading.
  - Options **B**, **D** and **E** have two segments shaded on the outside.
  - Options **A**, **B**, **D** and **E** have two segments shaded on the inside.
  - Options **A** and **B** have the shaded inner segments next to each other.
- Only option **B** fits all of the connections, so **B** is the correct answer.
- If you think that two options could be the correct answer you need to look for another connection, however subtle it might be.

> **Remember**
>
> This sort of question confuses a lot of people as often they don't look for enough connections. The way the inner segments are arranged is just as important as the number of inner segments that are shaded.

Moving and Connecting Shapes

- When shapes travel around the box, they can be moved in several different ways. The simplest movements are left to right or top to bottom.
- If you have two shapes they could swap places, and possibly sizes, at the same time. However, other types of change are when the shapes are joined up or put on top of each other.

Example

Look at the pair of images on the left connected by an arrow. Work out how the two images go together. Now look at the third image, which is followed by another arrow.

Work out which of the five images on the right completes the second pair in the same way as the first pair.

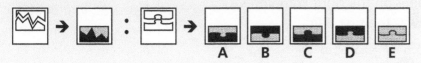

Linking Shapes Together

- Look closely at the first two images in the example above and see if you can work out what happens to get from the first to the second image:
  - The two sections are brought together.
  - They are rotated 180° as one.
  - The top section turns spotted.
  - The bottom section turns black.
  - The whole shape is moved to the bottom of the box.

Applying the Complete Relationship

- Once you have the relationship worked out, you need to take the third image and apply the changes to it **in the same order**:
  - The two sections are brought together.
  - They are rotated 180° as one.
  - The top section turns spotted.
  - The bottom section turns black.
  - The whole shape is moved to the bottom of the box.

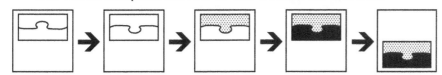

- The final image matches option **A**.

Reflections in Vertical Lines

- The most common type of reflection you will see is a reflection in a vertical line.
- Spotting these reflections is sometimes obvious as the shapes have all swapped sides. However, when there is just one shape in the box it may not be so obvious, as with the pentagon on the right.
- When a shape is reflected through a line, every point on the shape has to 'travel' to the line as quickly as possible, and then must 'continue' past the line for exactly the same distance.

Example
Look at the pair of images on the left connected by an arrow. Work out how the two images go together. Now look at the third image, which is followed by another arrow.

Work out which of the five images on the right completes the second pair in the same way as the first pair.

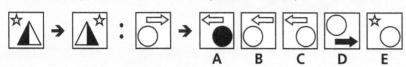

Recognising the Reflection Type
- There are two types of vertical reflection: one that happens **inside** the box and one that happens **between** boxes.
- Look closely at the first two images in the example and see if you can work out the type of reflection that is taking place:
  - The star moves from the left-hand side to the right-hand side.
  - The triangle moves from the right-hand side to the left-hand side.
  - The shaded section of the triangle moves from the left to the right.
  - It looks like everything has swapped over so the whole box has been reflected in a vertical mirror line.

Applying the Reflection to Another Image
- Now you will need to apply the reflection to the third image.
- Before looking at the possible answers, try to work out what it should look like:
  - The circle moves from the left to the right.
  - The arrow moves from the right to the left.
  - The arrow is reflected so it has to face the other way.
- The final image is a match for option **C**.

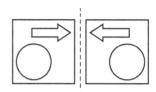

Reflections in Horizontal and Diagonal Lines

- Reflections in horizontal lines are often harder to spot than those in vertical lines.
- Look at the two pentagons shown right. The second one appears to be upside down compared to the first.

- If you think an image might be a reflection in a horizontal line, imagine that line is just below the box. Check by making points from the image 'travel' to that reflection line by the shortest route and then continue the same distance beyond it.
- One of the difficulties with reflections in a horizontal line is that the boxes are arranged side by side. However, you can sketch underneath the question:
  - Take each point of each shape to the line and then the same distance beyond.
  - Do this one shape at a time, and join the points up before doing the next shape.
  - Match what you have sketched to the answer options.
- The most complicated type of reflection is in a diagonal line. The reason is that it appears to make the different elements rotate and move in a way that doesn't quite seem right.

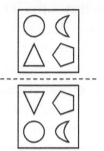

> **Example**
> Look at the pair of images on the left connected by an arrow. Work out how the two images go together. Now look at the third image, which is followed by another arrow. Work out which of the five images on the right completes the second pair in the same way as the first pair.
>
>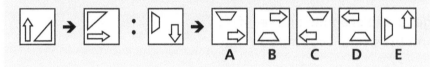
> A   B   C   D   E

Remember

Every point of each shape needs to reach the mirror line by the shortest possible route and continue the same distance beyond it. In the diagram below you can see an arrow where five of the corners have been marked with different colours. The arrow has been reflected in the diagonal line.

- Look closely at the first two images in the example and you will see that the two shapes almost seem to be moving to parts of the box independently of each other.
- The shapes have been reflected in a diagonal mirror line, drawn from bottom left to top right, across the box.

Applying a Reflection in a Diagonal Line to Another Image

- Now apply the reflection to the third image in the example. Use the coloured spot trick (shown on the right) to follow what is happening:
  - The mirror line is close to the bottom of the trapezium and to the top left corner of the arrow, so these parts of the shapes will not move as far as the rest.
  - The top of the trapezium and the right of the arrowhead will move the furthest.

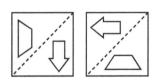

Remember

Squares and circles will always look the same once they have been reflected. If you put coloured spots on the corners of a square, you will be able to see that the reflection has happened.

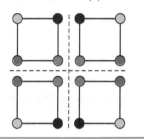

- The final image is a match for option **D**.

Rotations

- There are two aspects to rotations.
- The first is the direction of rotation, which can be clockwise or anti-clockwise. If the rotation is 180° it could be either clockwise or anti-clockwise (it comes to the same thing) and the direction is not important.
- The second aspect is the size of the rotation. Rotations take place in multiples of 45° or 60°, depending on the shape. With segmented shapes you will often notice that the rotation is of one or two segments, which can be easier to identify than a specific angle.

Example
Look at the pair of images on the left connected by an arrow. Work out how the two images go together. Now look at the third image, which is followed by another arrow.

Work out which of the five images on the right completes the second pair in the same way as the first pair.

- Look closely at the first two images in the example and see if you can work out the direction and the size of the rotation that is taking place.
  - The circle moves from bottom left to bottom right.
  - The arrow changes from pointing right to pointing up.
  - The arrowhead moves from top right to top left.
- It looks like the whole image has rotated 90° anti-clockwise.
- Once you are confident you have identified the rotation, you need to apply it to the third image to find the correct answer.
- If the arrow is rotated 90° anti-clockwise, it will go from pointing left to pointing down, with the head in the bottom right corner.
- If the parallelogram is rotated 90° anti-clockwise, it will go from the left to the bottom. There will be two vertical sides and two angled sides. The lowest point will be near the arrowhead.
- The correct answer is option **A**.

Working with Two Different Rotation Patterns
- Some questions might use two different rotation patterns. The shading of the outer segments could rotate in one direction while the shading of the inner segments could rotate in the other, as shown to the right.
- Another type of question uses a group of shapes with different shading patterns. The shapes might rotate around the box in one direction while the shading goes in the opposite direction, as shown to the right.

Quick Test

1. The two boxes on the left are a pair. Work out which of the five boxes on the right completes the second pair in the same way as the first pair.

a)  :

                    A   B   C   D   E

b)

                    A   B   C   D   E

2. There are two similar boxes on the left. Work out which of the five boxes on the right is most like the first two.

a) |

                    A   B   C   D   E

b) |

                    A   B   C   D   E

3. The two boxes on the left are a pair. Work out which of the five boxes on the right completes the second pair in the same way as the first pair.

a)   :

                    A   B   C   D   E

b)   :

                    A   B   C   D   E

4. The first two images on the left are a pair. Work out which of the five images on the right completes the second pair in the same way as the first pair.

a)   :

                    A   B   C   D   E

b)

                    A   B   C   D   E

5. The first two boxes on the left are a pair. Work out which of the five boxes on the right completes the second pair in the same way as the first pair.

a)   :

                    A   B   C   D   E

b)  :

                    A   B   C   D   E

c)  :

                    A   B   C   D   E

Spotting Patterns

You should be able to:

- identify the key box in 2 × 2 grids
- break down relationships to find the rules that are working within the grid
- identify vertical, horizontal and diagonal relationships within 3 × 3 grids
- discard irrelevant relationships and check that a potential relationship agrees.

Simple 2 × 2 Grids

- Simple 2 × 2 grid questions use all of the common connections and relationships, but the images that make up the question are arranged in a grid rather than in a line.
- In a 2 × 2 grid you will have three boxes with images and one that is blank. You need to work out which image should go into the empty box.

Example

One of the boxes is missing from the grid on the left. Work out which of the five boxes on the right completes the grid.

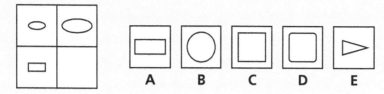

- Focus on the three boxes in the grid that have a shape inside them. Only one box is connected to the other two shapes – the box on the top left. This is the **key box**: it is the one that will help you unlock the answer.
- Now you need to look at how the shapes relate to the one in this key box:
  - The key box has a small oval in it. The oval is wider than its height.
  - The box to the right of the key box has a large oval in it. The oval is wider than its height.
  - The rule between these boxes is that the shape gets bigger as it goes from left to right.
- Now compare the box at the bottom left with the key box:
  - The key box has a small oval in it. The oval is wider than its height.
  - The box below the key box has a small rectangle in it. The rectangle is wider than its height.
  - The rule between these boxes is that the shape changes from an oval to a rectangle as it moves down the grid.
- Now that you have got the two rules, you should be able to work out which of the answers is correct:

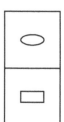

> **Remember**
>
> With simple 2 × 2 grid questions you can find that the answer is sometimes fairly obvious. However, take a few moments to double check it just in case there are two very similar possible answers. In the example on this page, options **C** and **D** look alike.

- The first rule suggests the small rectangle should become a large rectangle.
- The second rule suggests the large oval should become a large rectangle.

- The two rules suggest the answer is a large rectangle. The correct answer is option **A**.

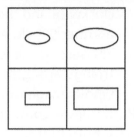

More Complex 2 × 2 Grids

- Complex 2 × 2 grid questions combine connections and relationships to make more complex rules.
- Just as with the simple grids, you need to look at the key box to unlock the question (the image connected to the other two).

Example

One of the boxes is missing from the grid on the left. Work out which of the five boxes on the right completes the grid.

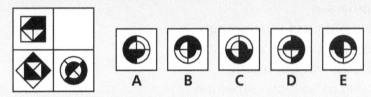

- The key box is at the bottom left.
- Look at how the other two images within the grid relate to the key box. You may need to look at the rule in more than one part.
- The key box has eight triangular segments in it, arranged to show a square inside a diamond. In the diamond the top and right segments are shaded black. In the square the bottom and left segments are shaded black.
- The box above the key box has eight triangular segments in it, arranged to show a diamond inside a square. In the square the two right-hand segments are shaded black. In the diamond the two top segments are shaded:
  - Looking at the whole image first, it appears to have rotated.
  - Looking at the outer segments, the shaded segments show the image has rotated 45° clockwise.
  - The shading in the inner segments has rotated more than the outer segments. It has rotated another 90° clockwise to make the new image.
- Now compare the box at the bottom right with the key box.
- The bottom-right box has eight segments that are all quarter circles. In the outer segments the right and bottom ones are shaded black. In the inner segments the top and left one are shaded black:
  - Looking at the whole image, the triangles have become circle segments, but the segments of both images seem to line up with each other.
  - The shaded segments have rotated 90° clockwise around the image.

- You could get the answer from using just one rule, but you should use both to check your answer:
  - The first rule suggests the circular image should rotate 45° clockwise and then the shaded inner segments should rotate another 90° clockwise.
  - The second rule suggests the top-left image should see the triangular segments become circular segments and then the whole image rotate 90° clockwise.
- Both rules suggest concentric circles. The outer one should have both bottom segments shaded black, while the inner one should have both right-hand segments shaded black.
- Option **C** is correct.

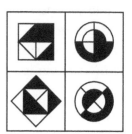

Simple 3 × 3 Grids

- In these questions you are shown nine boxes in a 3 × 3 grid and one of them is empty; you need to work out and pick the correct answer from the five options provided.
- The simpler questions will often involve rules and relationships that work in rows and columns. Sometimes it can be as simple as the shapes increasing in size as you go down the columns.
- Questions may involve a change of shading pattern or a reflection.

> **Example**
> One of the boxes is missing from the grid on the left. Work out which of the five boxes on the right completes the grid.

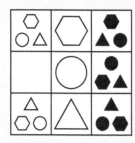 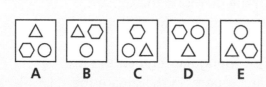

- There will be more than one relationship in the grid, even in simple questions. See how many relationships you can spot in the example above:
  - All of the shapes are hexagons, circles and equilateral triangles.
  - In the third column, all of the shapes are shaded black. The others are all shaded white.
  - In the third column, the position of the shapes rotates anti-clockwise within the squares.
  - In the first and third columns, there is always one shape above the other two.
  - The top shape in the first and third columns is the large shape in the middle column.
  - The first column appears to be a reflection of the third column with a shading change.

- Six different relationships is a lot for a simple question. However, with nine boxes in the grid you will often see this number of possibilities.
- Look at the relationships again: the first three can be ignored as all the answer options fit the first two and the third cannot apply to the first column.
- Now look at the possible answers the other three leave you with:
  - If there is always one shape above two others then only options **A**, **C** and **E** fit.
  - If the large shape is important then you want an answer with a circle at the top. Only option **E** fits.
  - If the reflection is important, the circle will be at the top and the other shapes underneath. Again only option **E** fits.
- All three of the rules give **E** as a possible option, with all of the other answers being proved incorrect by two of the rules.
- It is always worth double checking. The best way to do this is to sketch beside the grid, as keeping a lot of different relationships in your head can be tricky.
- Option **E** is the correct answer.

E

More Complex 3 × 3 Grids

- Complex 3 × 3 grid questions can involve relationships that work horizontally, vertically and diagonally.
- Some diagonal patterns can go in two different directions. For example, the shading pattern could run in the diagonal from top right to bottom left and the kind of shape from top left to bottom right.
- Rotational patterns are also quite common in this type of question.

Example
One of the boxes is missing from the grid on the left. Work out which of the five boxes on the right completes the grid.

A B C D E

- Complex grid questions may have fewer relationships than the simple questions, but they will be harder to spot. It can be useful to note when you **cannot** see a relationship.
- Have a look at the example above and see how many similarities and differences you can find:
  - All of the images look like teacups on saucers.
  - Some of the teacups appear to be facing the same direction.
  - There are no two teacups of the same shading pattern in any row or column.

- There are no two saucers of the same shading pattern in any row or column.
- There are no two pairs of saucers and teacups with the same shading pattern combination.
- The teacups with horizontal line shading appear to be in a diagonal line from top left to bottom right. The other teacups appear to follow that pattern.
- The saucer shading pattern appears to go from top right to bottom left.
- Quite a few of the relationships do not really give us any clue. It is only the last three rules that tell us what to look for:
  - If the teacup shading pattern is moving down and to the right, look for an image of a teacup with vertical stripes. Options **A**, **C** and **D** fit this.
  - If the saucer shading pattern is moving down and to the left, look for an image of a saucer with a hatched shading pattern. Options **B** and **D** fit this.
- These relationships might not seem to work together as they have focused on different parts of the image, but they do both agree on one of the possible options: **D**.
- To check that option **D** is right, you should sketch beside the grid. Start by drawing a saucer and teacup as the basic shape is always the same. Then apply the shading for the teacup and follow that with the shading for the saucer. Compare your sketch with the possible answers.
- Option **D** is the correct answer.

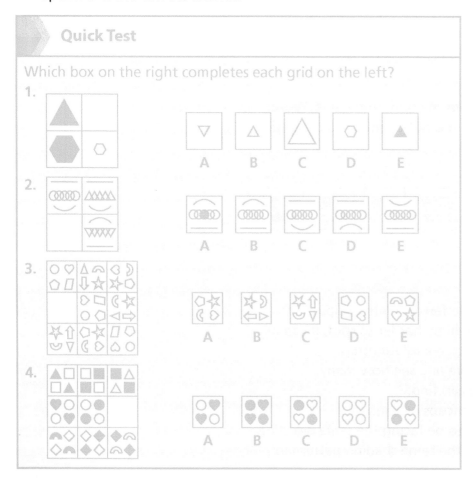

Completing Sequences

You should be able to:

- identify repeating patterns that alternate, reflect or rotate
- identify all the connections in a pattern with repeating steps
- recognise a number pattern and identify the increase or decrease from one box to the next
- solve problems with square and triangular number sequences.

Repeating Patterns

- Repeating patterns questions use one relationship repetitively between the five boxes on the left.
- These are simple patterns and often include just two images that keep swapping, like a triangle becoming a circle and then going back to a triangle.

> **Example**
> Find which one of the five boxes on the right completes the sequence or pattern on the left.
>
>

- Looking at the example above:
  - The first, third and fifth boxes have happy faces.
  - The second box has a sad face.
- To follow this pattern, the empty box should be identical to the second box.
- You are looking for a sad face with no shading, which is option **C**.
- This is an example of a simple alternating pattern.

Identifying Reflecting Patterns

- Other patterns are based on reflections.
- Look at the three triangles on the right and work out what sort of reflection is happening between each pair of boxes:

  - The first box has a right-angled triangle with the right angle in the bottom left of the box.
  - The second box has a similar right-angled triangle with the right angle in the bottom right of the box.
  - The third box matches the first box.
- As you work from left to right, the shape is being reflected in a vertical mirror line.
- Sometimes the repeating pattern is not as obvious as you might expect.

- Look at these five boxes and work out where the reflection is in this question:

  - All of the shapes are regular.
  - The first and last boxes match each other.
- The reflection is a vertical mirror line that goes through the middle of the third box and straight through the triangle inside it.
- These sorts of patterns build up in the first three boxes before reversing in the last three boxes. The middle box is always unique.

Identifying Extended Patterns

- Another common repeating pattern involves rotation.
- In these questions, the image will rotate a set amount from box to box, eventually returning to its original position. The pattern will then repeat.
- Look at these five boxes and work out what is happening in each box:

- Since the two 'arms' of the image are of different length, the rotation is easy to follow. The image rotates 90° clockwise between the boxes. The pattern repeats every four boxes.
- Whenever you have a pattern like this with a 90° rotation, the first and last boxes will always match each other as long as there are no additional connections such as a shading pattern change.

One-Step Patterns

- One-step pattern questions have one relationship that is used repeatedly between the five boxes on the left.
- It could be that something – the same item or the same amount – is added each time. It could also be a combination of items, but the key here is that you are looking for the same change every time.

Example
Find which one of the five boxes on the right completes the sequence or pattern on the left.

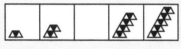
A   B   C   D   E

- In the example the third box is missing, and this can be the most difficult one as three boxes in a row can make patterns easier to spot.
- Have a look at the other images and see if you can identify the pattern:
  - The first box has three triangles in it, one black and two white.
  - The second box has double the number of triangles in it, with the same proportion of black and white.
  - The fourth box has four times the number of triangles as the first box, with the same proportion of black and white.
  - The fifth box has five times the number of triangles as the first box, with the same proportion of black and white.
- It looks like the third box should have three times the number of triangles, with the same proportion of black and white.
- Unfortunately, a few of the possible options fit this explanation so you need to find something else.
- Look again at how the triangles are arranged:
  - The three triangles in the first box are in a line with the middle one upside down. Treat this as the basic block.
  - The other images are made up of similar blocks on top of each other. The bottom block is always in the same place and they are arranged so that there is a straight line running up the left-hand side.
- You are now looking for three blocks, starting in the bottom-left corner with a smooth line on the left-hand side and one black triangle for every two white triangles:
  - Option **A** does not have three rows.
  - Option **B** fits all of the connections you have found.
  - Option **C** does not have the straight line on the left-hand side.
  - Option **D** has the wrong proportion of black and white shading.
  - Option **E** is in the wrong place.
- The correct answer is option **B**.

Two- and Three-Step Patterns

- Two-step patterns have two distinct changes taking place. Sometimes one change is a shape being built up, while the other is another shape being reduced. Usually both changes happen in each box, but sometimes one of the changes only happens in every other box, just to catch you out.
- Three-step patterns are an extension of two-step patterns but with three distinct changes taking place. You need to approach them in exactly the same way as two-step patterns, but find three different connections.

> **Remember**
>
> It can be very easy to spot a pattern and get carried away, so take a few moments with these questions – check the shading patterns are not swapping, or the positions are not changing.

> **Remember**
>
> One-step patterns are one of the question types where you are unlikely to see extra shapes in the box to distract you.

Example

Find which one of the five boxes on the right completes the sequence or pattern on the left.

- As two-step patterns have at least two different connections, it is a good idea to work on one at a time. The example above has two parts – the inverted V shapes and the lines:
  - An extra inverted V is added to each box. These start on the left and are all connected to make a zigzag pattern.
  - The first box has six lines at the top and none at the bottom.
  - The second box has five lines at the top and one at the bottom.
  - The third box has four lines at the top and two at the bottom.
- It looks like one of the lines is moving from the top to the bottom in each box. You can use the fifth box to check this. It should have two lines at the top and four at the bottom. It does, so you have found the rule.
- It is very easy to find some connections and believe you have found all of them, but always double-check. The best way to do this is to mark the question with a different symbol for each connection – a dot, a short vertical line, a short horizontal line or another similar simple mark.
- Now you need to work out what should be in the empty box:
  - There should be four inverted V shapes in the middle.
  - There should be three lines at the top and three lines at the bottom.
- The correct answer is option **C**.

> **Remember**

These questions are all about the little details. In the example here, look at the way the inverted V shapes start on the left and grow across the boxes, but are always linked together. Also have a look at the lines. While one line always moves to the bottom, the lowest one from the top moves to become the highest line at the bottom. Only one line moves at a time.

Simple Number Patterns

- Simple number patterns are all about the number of shapes, sides or corners in each image and the way they increase or decrease. This will generally be a change of one or two per box, but the change is the same in every box.
- You have probably seen sequences like 1, 3, 5, 7, 9 and that is exactly the sort of pattern you will see in this sort of question.
- Patterns are based on addition, subtraction or multiplication, although multiplication is rarer.

Example

Find which one of the five boxes on the right completes the sequence or pattern on the left.

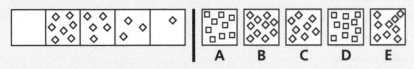

- Look at the images above and see if you can work out the pattern:
  - The first box is empty.
  - The second box has seven diamonds in it.
  - The third box has five diamonds in it.
  - The fourth box has three diamonds in it.
  - The fifth box has one diamond in it.
- The number of diamonds is decreasing by two as you move from left to right. That means two diamonds are added as you go from right to left.
- As the second box has seven diamonds in it, you need to find an answer with 7 + 2 = 9 diamonds:
  - Option **A** has nine squares in it.
  - Option **B** has ten diamonds in it.
  - Option **C** has eight diamonds in it.
  - Option **D** has ten squares in it.
  - Option **E** has nine diamonds in it.
- The diamonds in the example are just squares that have been rotated 45°, but in all of the boxes in the question the diamonds are identical so the correct answer is option **E**.

Square Number Patterns

- A square number is what you get when you multiply a number by itself:
  - 2 × 2 = 4 means that 4 is a square number.
  - The first 10 square numbers are 1, 4, 9, 16, 25, 36, 49, 64, 81 and 100.
- Questions that use square number patterns will often have lots of small shapes, with each box having a square number of shapes. The sequence could be increasing or decreasing.

Example

Find which one of the five boxes on the right completes the sequence or pattern on the left.

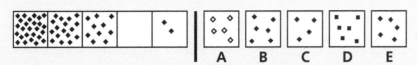

- Look at the five boxes in the pattern above and make a note of the contents of each one:
  - The first box has 26 black diamonds in it.

> **Remember**
>
> One of the great things about simple number patterns is that you can usually work out what you are looking for quickly.

> **Remember**
>
> One of the answer options may have the right number of the wrong shape, so make sure you are focusing on the whole question and not just the number sequence.

> **Remember**
>
> Sometimes there could be another connection on top of the square number pattern, such as the shapes changing from one box to another or a rotation.

- The second box has 17 black diamonds in it.
- The third box has 10 black diamonds in it.
- The fourth box is empty.
- The fifth box has two black diamonds in it.
- Ignore the last box for now and focus on the first three:
    - To get from 26 to 17 you take away nine.
    - To get from 17 to 10 you take away seven.
- The difference appears to be decreasing by two each time.
- If the difference between boxes is decreasing by two each time, then five shapes must be removed from the third box to get the fourth box. In turn, three shapes must be removed from the fourth box.
- You need to ask if that will leave two shapes in the last box:
    - Box three has 10 black diamonds in it. Removing five would leave five black diamonds in the empty box.
    - If you now take away three from the remaining five, you will be left with two black diamonds in the last box, which matches what you can see.
- The correct answer must have five black diamonds in the box. Option **E** is the only possible answer.

Triangular Number Patterns

- The sequence of triangular numbers is based on adding up all of the whole numbers from 1 to whichever triangular number you want:
    - To get the third triangular number you have to do the sum 1 + 2 + 3 = 6.
    - The first 10 triangular numbers are 1, 3, 6, 10, 15, 21, 28, 36, 45 and 55.
- Questions that use triangular numbers work in the same way as those with square numbers.

Example
Find which one of the five boxes on the right completes the sequence or pattern on the left.

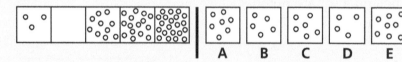

- Have a look at the five boxes above and make a note of the contents of each one:
    - The first box has three circles.
    - The second box is empty.
    - The third box has 10 circles.
    - The fourth box has 15 circles.
    - The fifth box has 21 circles.

Remember

If the number of shapes in each box increases by two more than the previous increase, you have a square number sequence.

Remember

If you have discounted an answer, put a little faint cross at the top to help yourself remember.

Remember

The boxes in the questions can only hold a limited number of shapes, so you are unlikely to have to remember more than the sequence of triangular numbers to 28.

- Ignore the first box for now and focus on the last three:
  - To get from 10 to 15 you have to add five.
  - To get from 15 to 21 you have to add six.
- The difference appears to be increasing by one each time.
- If the difference is increasing by one each time, then the difference between the second and third boxes must be four, and from the second to the first box it must be three.
- You need to ask if that gives the correct number of circles in the first box:
  - Box three has 10 circles in it. If you take away four, you would have six circles in the second box.
  - If you take away three from the six, you are left with three circles in the first box, which is correct.
- The correct answer must have six circles in the box. Option **C** is the only possible answer.
- You might have noticed that the sequence in the boxes is part of the triangular number sequence 1, 3, 6, 10, 15... and so worked out straight away that the number of circles in the second box must be six.
- However, this wouldn't have been so easy to see if this sequence had been, for example, 4, 6, 9, 13, 18 (with one number missing).

> **Remember**
>
> If the number of shapes in each box increases by one more than the previous increase, you have a triangular number sequence.

Quick Test

Which of the images on the right can be used to complete the sequence in the boxes on the left?

1.
   A B C D E

2.
   A B C D E

3.
   A B C D E

4.
   A B C D E

5.
   A B C D E

6.
   A B C D E

7.
   A B C D E

Spatial Reasoning

You should be able to:

- identify how nets of cubes look when they are folded
- imagine how holes punched in folded paper would look when they are unfolded
- find hidden shapes and make shapes using 2D figures
- imagine rotating figures made out of groups of blocks
- imagine how groups of blocks would look when viewed from different angles.

Nets and Cubes

- Nets and cubes questions will show you an image of a net and the answer options will consist of five cubes.
- You will need to identify which of the cubes could be made from the given net.
- This is an example of a typical cubes and nets question:

Example
Look at the net. Which of the cubes could be made from the net shown?

> **Remember**
>
> Sometimes these questions will ask you which cube could **not** be made from the given net, or which net could be used to make a given cube. They all require the same skills and techniques. Read the question carefully to make sure you do what it is asking.

- Looking at the example above:
  - The oval and the square are opposite when the net is folded.
  - The rectangle and the heart are opposite when the net is folded.
  - The diamond and the circle are opposite when the net is folded.
- You can eliminate option **A** because the concentric circles do not appear on the net.
- You can eliminate options **C** and **E** because they show faces which are opposite one another.
- You can eliminate option **B** because the heart touches the diamond with the curved part of the heart rather than the point.
- The heart, square and circle can touch one another as shown in option **D**.
- In all, there are 11 different nets that can be used to make a cube so any of these could appear in a question:

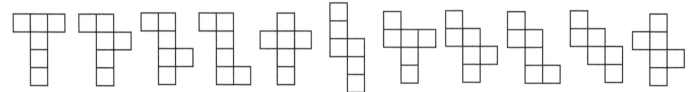

- Make sure you know how all these different nets would fold into a cube.

Paper Folding and Hole Punching

- Paper folding and hole punching questions will show you a square piece of paper that has been folded several times.
- You will see that the paper has then had holes punched in it.
- You will need to work out what the unfolded paper would look like when it is opened out.

> **Example**
> Look at the square piece of paper below. It is folded and holes are punched in it. What would it look like when it is unfolded?
>
>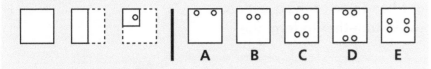
>
>   A   B   C   D   E

- In the example above, the paper has been folded in half vertically so both layers are on the left-hand side.
- It has then been folded upwards into a quarter with all four layers of paper in the top left-hand corner of the original square.
- Imagine the paper being unfolded, carrying out the reverse of what has been done. Try to imagine the holes appearing as the paper unfolds one step at a time:
  - First the paper would unfold downwards so there would be two holes, aligned vertically:
  - Then the paper would be unfolded again so the holes would be symmetrical in two vertically aligned columns:
- Therefore the correct answer option is **C**.

Hidden Shapes

- Hidden shapes questions give a figure on the left-hand side and ask you to find that figure within one of the answer options given on the right.
- The shape might be rotated in the correct answer option but it will not change in size or be reflected.
- Below is an example of a hidden shapes question:

> **Example**
> Look at the given shape. It is hidden in one of the images A–E. In which image is the shape hidden?
>
>
>
>   A   B   C   D   E

- In this example, the figure given on the left-hand side of the question is hidden in answer option **A**:

Make a Shape (2D)

- Make a shape (2D) tasks require you to look at a group of figures on the left-hand side of the question.
- You will need to imagine moving these figures to make one of the large shapes shown on the right-hand side of the question.
- The figures can be rotated and pushed together to form the larger shape.

Example

Which of the shapes on the right could be made from the figures on the left?

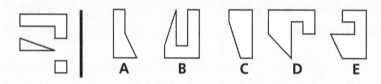

> **Remember**
>
> The figures on the left-hand side can be rotated to form the large shape on the right, but not reduced, enlarged or reflected.

- In the example above, the three figures could be rotated to make the shape in option **B**, so that is the correct answer:

- Shapes on the right-hand side which would require extra figures in addition to those on the left cannot be correct. Here, the extra figure marked in grey would be needed to make option **D**, and the triangular piece would need reflecting, so that cannot be correct:

Rotating 3D Block Figures

- Rotating figures made of 3D blocks requires you to look at a given set of figures made from different arrangements of blocks.
- You will need to imagine the figures have been rotated and match up each figure with its rotation.
- The figures can be rotated around the horizontal axis or turned around the vertical axis, but the blocks in each figure cannot be altered or change positions.

Revision

Example

Here are three figures, **A**, **B** and **C**:

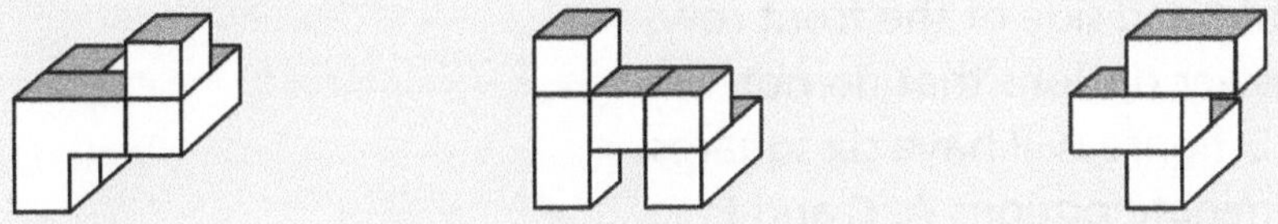

A   B   C

The figures are rotated and the rotations are shown below. Match each rotation to the original figure.

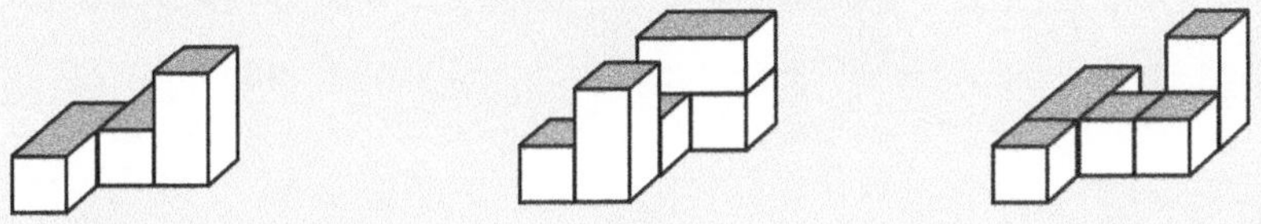

i   ii   iii

> **Remember**
>
> The best way to practise these questions is to test yourself using actual blocks. You can make figures using toy blocks and see how they look from different angles or when they are turned.

- In the example above, the first rotation (i) shows figure **C** rotated and turned forwards.
- The second rotation (ii) shows figure **A** rotated and turned forwards.
- The third rotation (iii) shows figure **B** turned forwards.

Plans and Elevations

- Plans and elevations questions will show you a figure made up of 3D blocks.
- You will need to imagine looking at the figure from another angle (usually from above) and you will need to select the answer option that shows a 2D view of this.
- Picture the figure from the new perspective by looking carefully at how the 3D blocks are arranged, their shape and their size.
- Consider all the answer options before selecting the one that shows the 2D view of the given figure.

> **Remember**
>
> Always double check whether you are being asked to find the view of the figure from above (the 'plan' view) or from the front or a side (an 'elevation').

Example

Look at the given figure. Select the answer option which shows the top-down (plan) view of the figure.

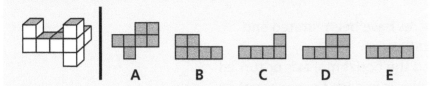

- In this example, you can see that the front row of 3D blocks, nearest to you as you are looking at the figure, has four blocks when viewed from above.
- The second row of blocks, at the back as you look at the figure, has two blocks aligned with the right-hand side of the front row.
- Therefore, you can eliminate all answer options that do not have a total of six squares, as the 3D figure will have six squares visible in the plan view. You can eliminate options **A**, **C** and **E**.
- To choose between options **B** and **D**, you need to select the answer with the second row squares aligned to the right-hand side of the first row.
- Therefore, the correct answer is option **D**.
- Make sure you take into account any lower blocks which would be visible in a plan view:

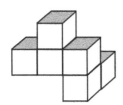

- Here the block at the back right-hand side of the figure would show on the plan view, even though it is lower in height than the other blocks:

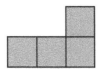

Quick Test

1. Look at each net below. Select which cube (**A, B, C, D** or **E**) could be made from each net.

a)

                     A   B   C   D   E

b)

                     A   B   C   D   E

2. Look at the given shape on the left of each question. Choose the image (**A, B, C, D** or **E**) in which this shape is hidden.

a)

                     A   B   C   D   E

b)

                     A   B   C   D   E

3. Look at each square of paper, which has been folded and holes punched through.

Select the answer option (**A, B, C, D** or **E**) which shows how the square would appear when it is unfolded.

a)

                         A   B   C   D   E

b)

                         A   B   C   D   E

4. Match shapes **A, B** and **C** to their rotations **i, ii** and **iii** below.

    A   B   C

    i   ii   iii

THIS PAGE HAS DELIBERATELY BEEN LEFT BLANK

Collins

11+
Non-Verbal Reasoning

Practice

Workbook

Look at the five images in each row. Work out what connects **four** of the images and makes the other image the odd one out. Find the image **most unlike** the others.

Example

A　　　　　B　　　　　C　　　　　D　　　　　E

Shapes A, C, D and E all have four sides; shape B has three sides.
The shape most unlike the others is **B**.

Now have a go at these similar questions. Find the image **most unlike** the others.

1

A　　　　　B　　　　　C　　　　　D　　　　　E

2

A　　　　　B　　　　　C　　　　　D　　　　　E

3

A　　　　　B　　　　　C　　　　　D　　　　　E

4

A　　　　　B　　　　　C　　　　　D　　　　　E

5

A　　　　　B　　　　　C　　　　　D　　　　　E

Look at the two images on the left. Decide what makes these two images similar to each other. Now find the image on the right **most like** the two images on the left.

Example 2

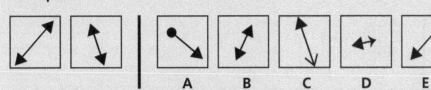

The two images on the left have identical arrowheads at both ends of the line. Only **B** has the same arrowhead at both ends.

Now have a go at these similar questions. Find the image (A, B, C, D or E) **most like** those on the left.

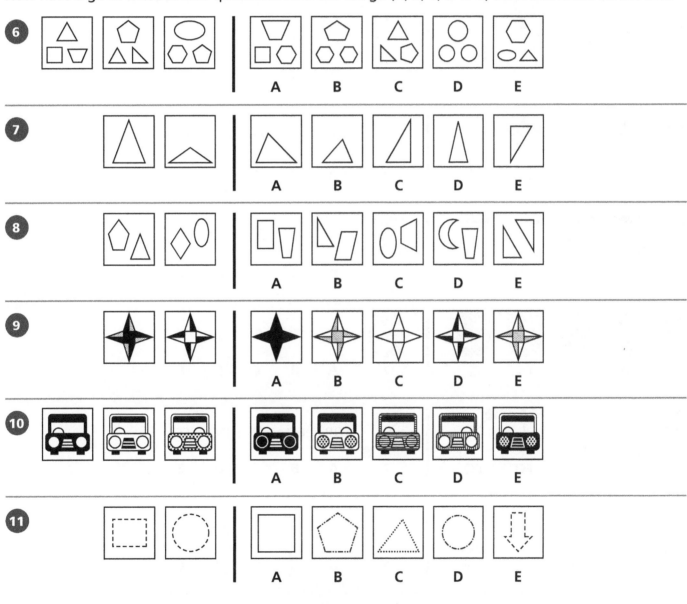

END OF TEST

The four images on the left each have a code. Work out how the codes go with these images. Now find the correct code from the list on the right that matches the fifth image.

Example

KR	LS	KT	MR		?	KS	LT	MT	LR	MS
						A	B	C	D	E

The fifth shape is a circle and has a hatched pattern. A circle has the letter code L. A hatched pattern has the letter code T. The answer is **B**.

Now have a go at these similar questions. Find the code that matches the fifth image.

1

AN	CP	AO	BN		?	CO	BP	AP	BO	CN
						A	B	C	D	E

2

DS	FT	ES	DR		?	FR	ET	ER	FS	DT
						A	B	C	D	E

3

PT	PS	QU	RT		?	QS	RU	PU	QT	RP
						A	B	C	D	E

4

GK	EJ	FK	EL		?	GJ	EK	FJ	GL	FL
						A	B	C	D	E

5

EP	DQ	FO	EQ		?	DP	EO	FP	DO	FQ
						A	B	C	D	E

6

VA	UC	VB	WA		?	UA	WB	VC	WC	UB
						A	B	C	D	E

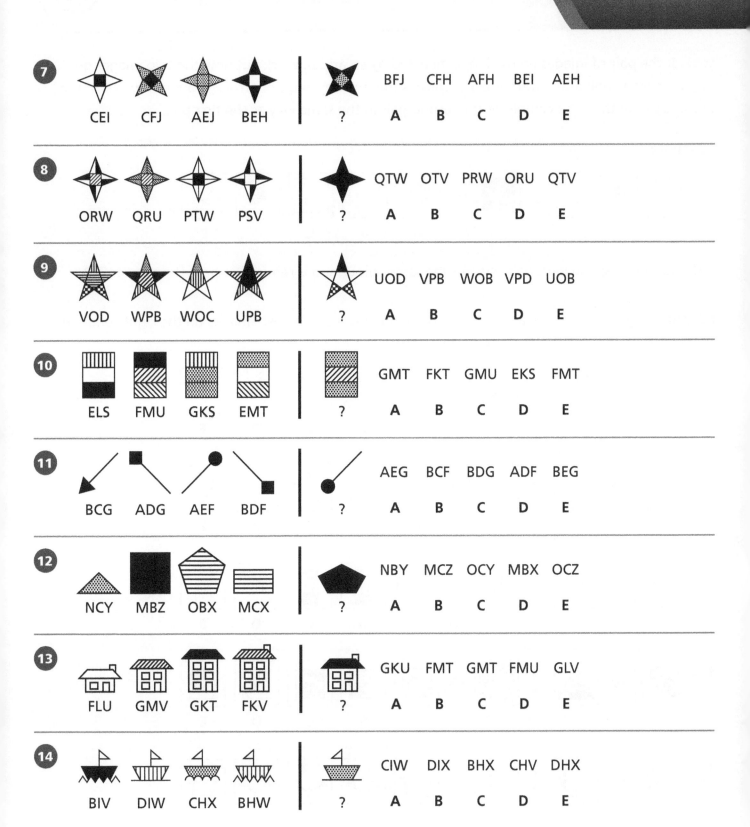

7

CEI   CFJ   AEJ   BEH

	BFJ	CFH	AFH	BEI	AEH
?	A	B	C	D	E

8

ORW   QRU   PTW   PSV

	QTW	OTV	PRW	ORU	QTV
?	A	B	C	D	E

9

VOD   WPB   WOC   UPB

	UOD	VPB	WOB	VPD	UOB
?	A	B	C	D	E

10

ELS   FMU   GKS   EMT

	GMT	FKT	GMU	EKS	FMT
?	A	B	C	D	E

11

BCG   ADG   AEF   BDF

	AEG	BCF	BDG	ADF	BEG
?	A	B	C	D	E

12

NCY   MBZ   OBX   MCX

	NBY	MCZ	OCY	MBX	OCZ
?	A	B	C	D	E

13

FLU   GMV   GKT   FKV

	GKU	FMT	GMT	FMU	GLV
?	A	B	C	D	E

14

BIV   DIW   CHX   BHW

	CIW	DIX	BHX	CHV	DHX
?	A	B	C	D	E

END OF TEST

Look at the pair of images on the left, connected by an arrow. Work out how the two images go together. Now look at the third image, which is followed by another arrow. Work out which of the five images on the right completes the second pair in the same way as the first pair.

Example

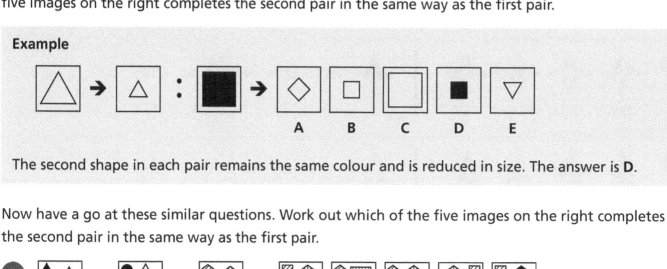

The second shape in each pair remains the same colour and is reduced in size. The answer is **D**.

Now have a go at these similar questions. Work out which of the five images on the right completes the second pair in the same way as the first pair.

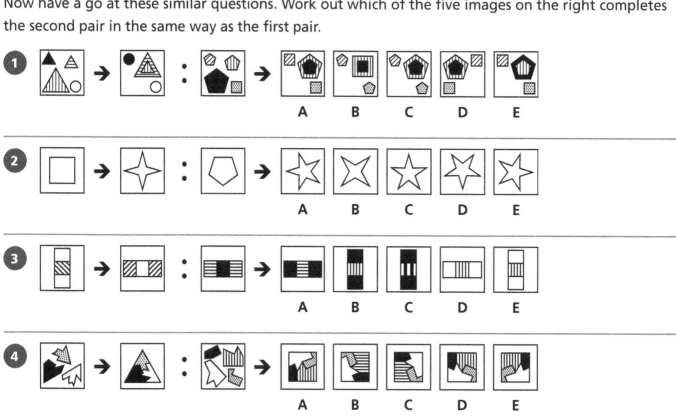

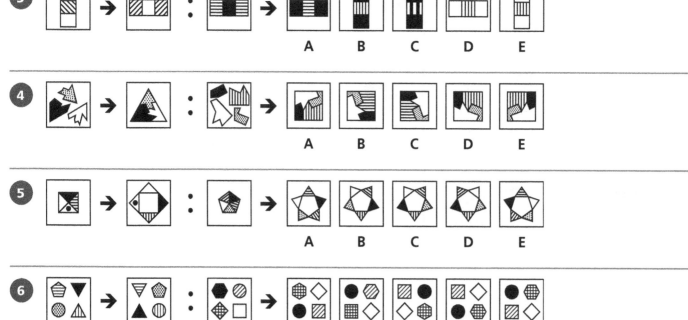

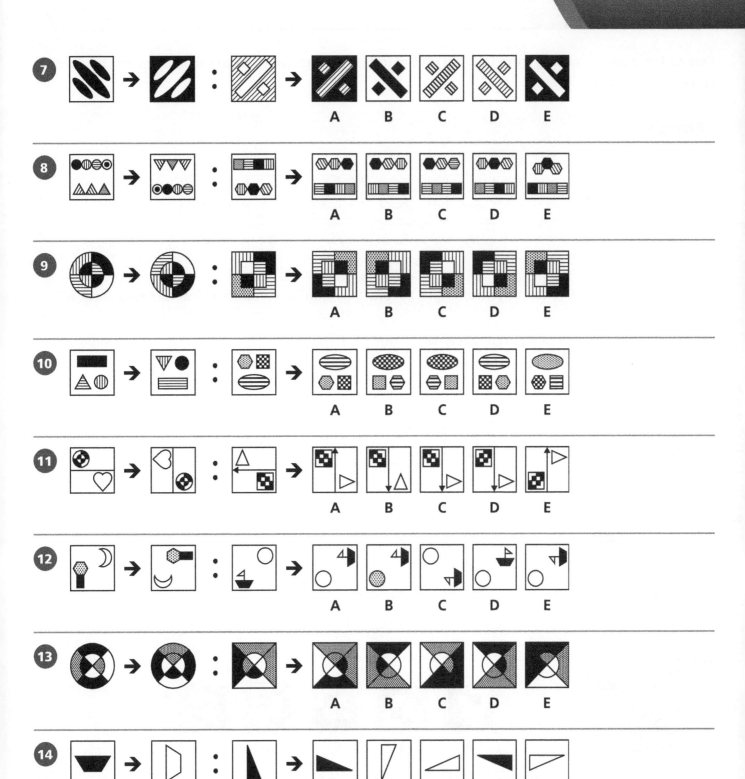

One of the boxes is missing from the grid on the left. Work out which of the five boxes on the right completes the grid.

Example

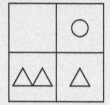

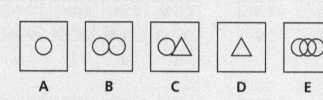

As the shapes in the boxes move from right to left, they double in number. The correct answer is **B**.

Now have a go at these similar questions. Work out which of the five boxes on the right completes the grid.

1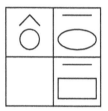

      A   B   C   D   E

2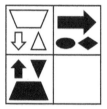

      A   B   C   D   E

3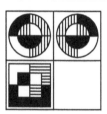

      A   B   C   D   E

4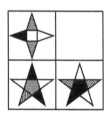

      A   B   C   D   E

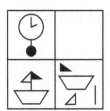

A   B   C   D   E

A   B   C   D   E

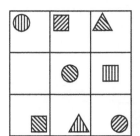

A   B   C   D   E

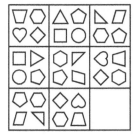

A   B   C   D   E

END OF TEST

Find which one of the five boxes on the right completes the sequence or pattern on the left.

Example

Looking at the boxes from left to right, the number of sides on the shape increases by one each time. The correct answer is **C**.

Now have a go at these similar questions. Find which one of the five boxes on the right completes the sequence or pattern on the left.

1

    A   B   C   D   E

2

    A   B   C   D   E

3

    A   B   C   D   E

4

    A   B   C   D   E

5

    A   B   C   D   E

6

    A   B   C   D   E

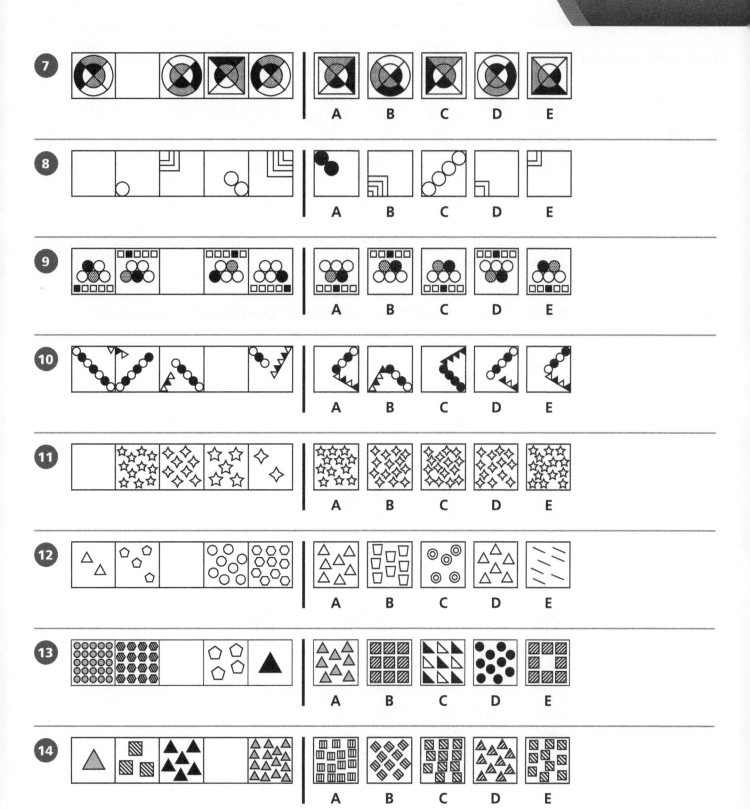

END OF TEST

Look at the given net. Select the answer option that shows the cube that can be made from the given net.

Example

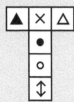

A   **B**   **C**   **D**   **E**

The double-headed arrow will point to the cross and the white circle. The triangle will point to the double-headed arrow. Therefore the answer is **C**.

Now have a go at these similar questions. Select the cube that can be made from the given net.

1

    A   **B**   **C**   **D**   **E**

2

    A   **B**   **C**   **D**   **E**

3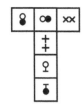

    A   **B**   **C**   **D**   **E**

4

    A   **B**   **C**   **D**   **E**

5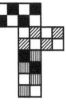

    A   **B**   **C**   **D**   **E**

Look at the shape in each question. It is hidden in one of the answer options A, B, C, D or E. Select the answer option in which the given shape is hidden.

Example

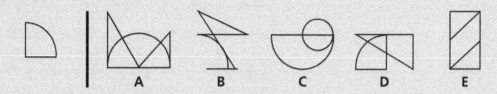

The hidden shape is a quarter circle. It appears only in option D, so **D** is the correct answer.

Now have a go at these similar questions. Select the answer option in which the given shape is hidden.

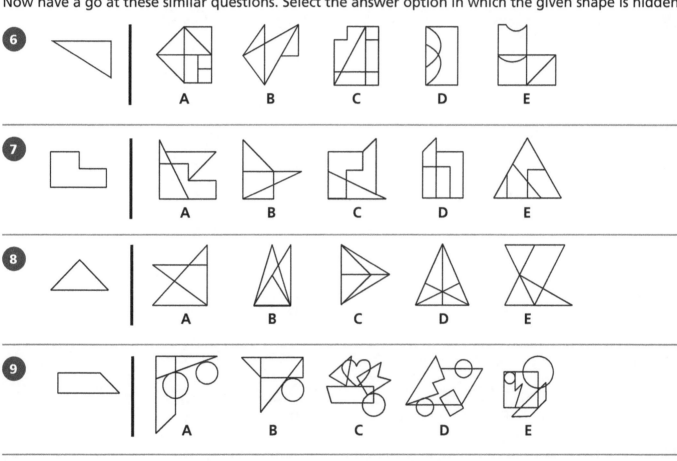

END OF TEST

Look at the five images in each row. Work out what connects **four** of the images and makes the other image the odd one out. Find the image **most unlike** the others.

Example

Shapes A, C, D and E all have four sides; shape B has three sides. The shape most unlike the others is **B**.

Now have a go at these similar questions. Find the image that is **most unlike** the others.

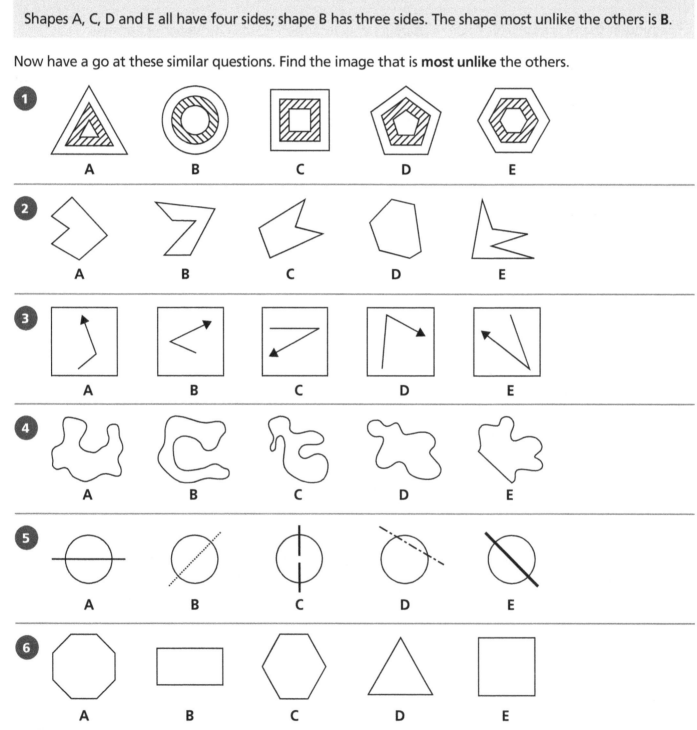

The four images on the left each have a code. Work out how the codes go with these images. Now find the correct code from the list on the right that matches the fifth image.

Example

The fifth shape is a circle and has a hatched pattern. A circle has the letter code L. A hatched pattern has the letter code T. The answer is **B**.

Now have a go at these similar questions. Find the code that matches the fifth image.

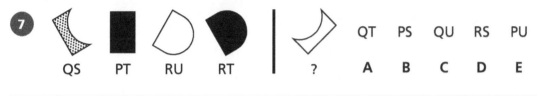

Look at the pair of images on the left, connected by an arrow. Work out how the two images go together. Now look at the third image, which is followed by another arrow. Work out which of the five images on the right completes the second pair in the same way as the first pair.

Example

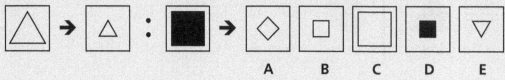

The second shape in each pair remains the same colour and is reduced in size. The answer is **D**.

Now have a go at these similar questions. Work out which of the five images on the right completes the second pair in the same way as the first pair.

12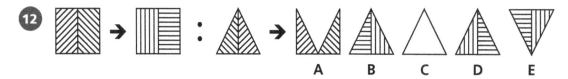

13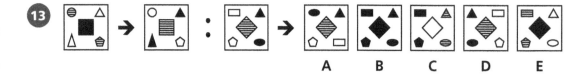

14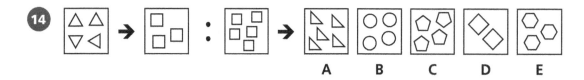

15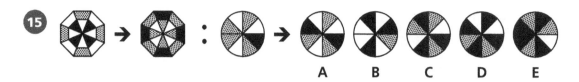

16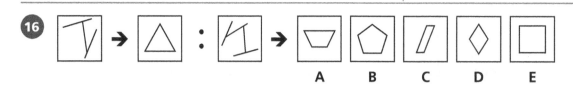

17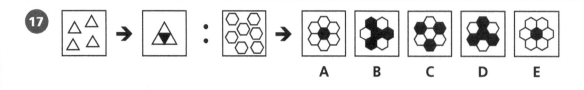

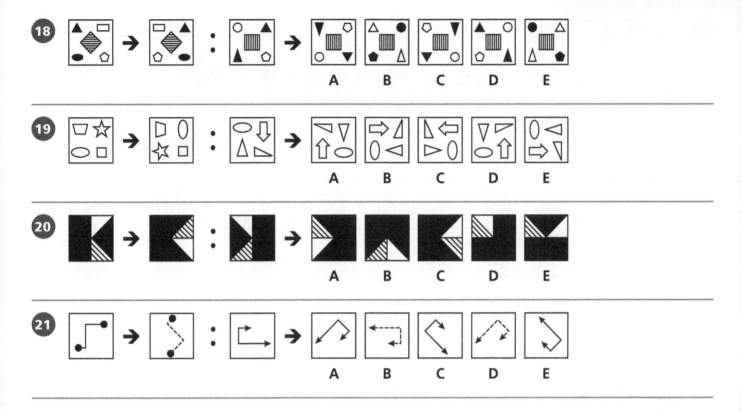

18 A B C D E

19 A B C D E

20 A B C D E

21 A B C D E

One of the boxes is missing from the grid on the left. Work out which of the five boxes on the right completes the grid.

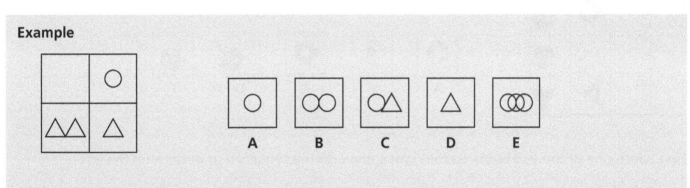

Example

As the shapes in the boxes move from right to left, they double in number. The correct answer is **B**.

Now have a go at these similar questions. Work out which of the five boxes on the right completes the grid.

22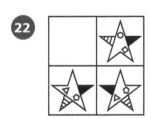

A B C D E

23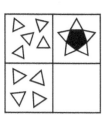

A   B   C   D   E

24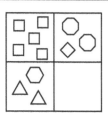

A   B   C   D   E

25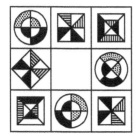

A   B   C   D   E

26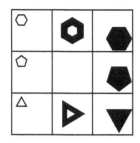

A   B   C   D   E

Find which one of the five boxes on the right completes the sequence or pattern on the left.

Example

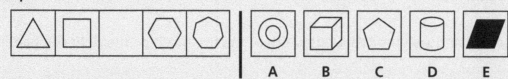

Looking at the boxes from left to right, the number of sides on the shape increases by one each time. The correct answer is **C**.

Now have a go at these similar questions. Find which one of the five boxes on the right completes the sequence or pattern on the left.

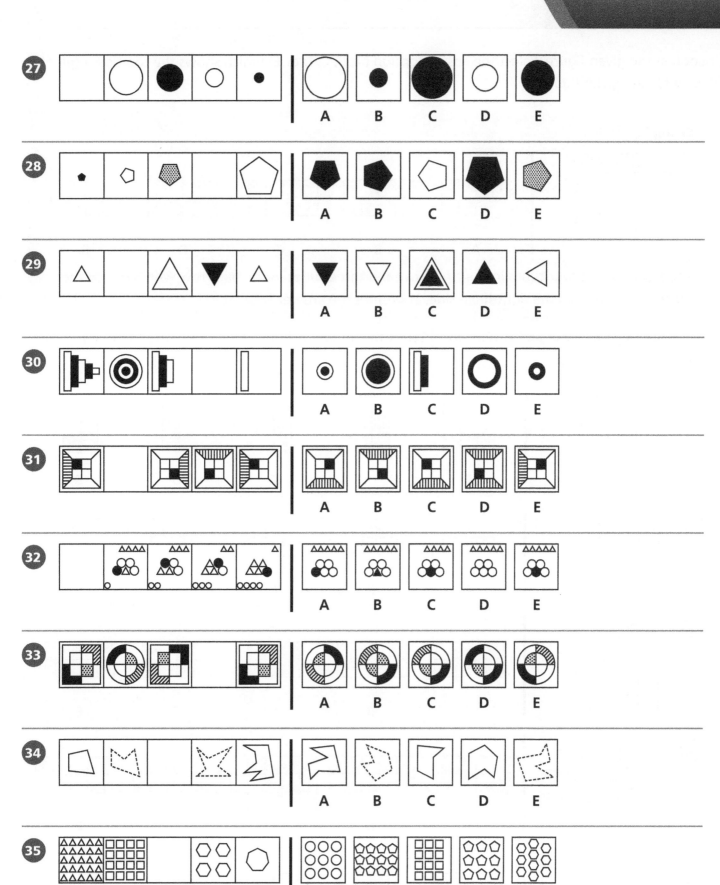

Look at the given figure. Select the answer option (A, B, C, D or E) which shows the top-down (plan) view for the given figure.

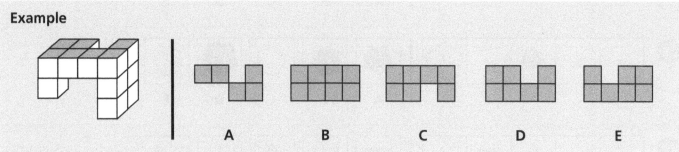

Example

A   B   C   D   E

The figure shows four cubes in the front row and three cubes in the back row with a gap in the second column from the right-hand side. Therefore the answer is **D**.

Now have a go at these similar questions. Select the answer option which shows the top-down (plan) view for the given figure.

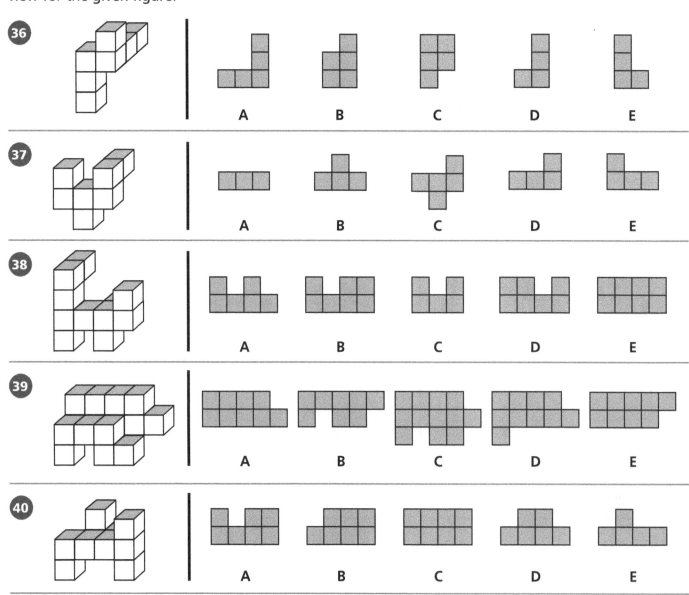

Look at the square of paper shown on the left. Look at how it has been folded and some holes punched through. Imagine the paper has been unfolded. Select the answer option that shows what it would look like.

Example

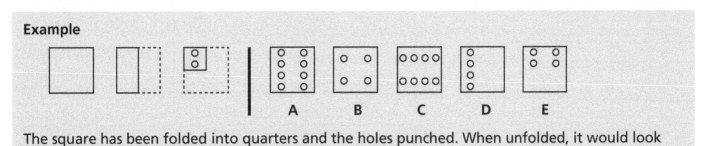

The square has been folded into quarters and the holes punched. When unfolded, it would look like option **A**, so this is the correct answer.

Now have a go at these similar questions. Each square on the left has been folded and holes punched through. Select the option that shows how it would look when unfolded.

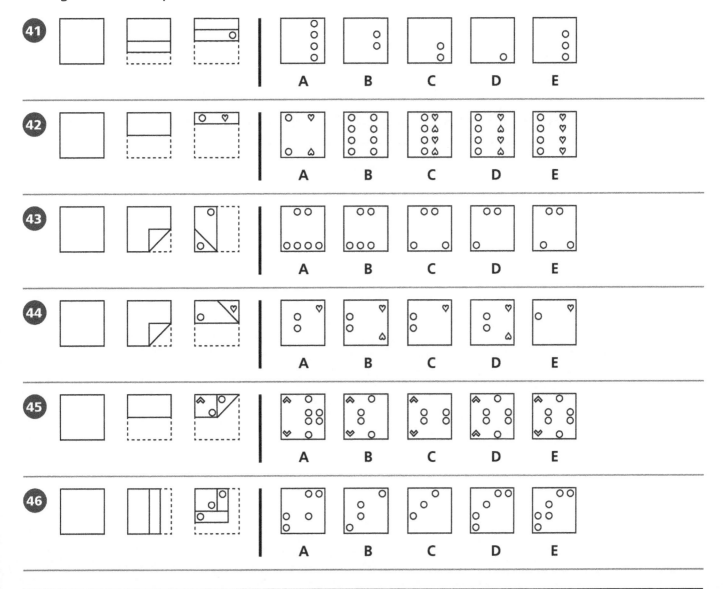

END OF TEST

THIS PAGE HAS DELIBERATELY BEEN LEFT BLANK

Collins

11+

Non-Verbal Reasoning

Assessment

Workbook

THIS PAGE HAS DELIBERATELY BEEN LEFT BLANK

Collins

Non-Verbal Reasoning Multiple Choice Practice Paper 1

Read these instructions carefully:

1. You must not open or turn over this booklet until you are told to do so.

2. The booklet contains a multiple-choice test, in which you have to mark your answer to each question on the separate answer sheet.

3. There are five sections in this test. Each section starts with an explanation of what to do, followed by an example. You will then be asked to do some practice questions. Explanations of the answers for these are included.

4. You should indicate one answer only for each question by drawing a firm pencil line clearly through the rectangle next to your answer on the answer sheet. Rub out any mistakes as well as you can and put in your new answer.

5. Complete the questions as quickly and as carefully as you can. If you find that you cannot do a question, do not waste time on it but go on to the next one.

6. You have 6 minutes to complete the 12 questions in each section.

7. You should do any rough working on a separate sheet of paper.

Section 1

In the example below are two images on the left with an arrow between them. Then there is a third image with an arrow pointing to five more images. Decide which one of these five images goes with the third image to make a pair like the two on the left.

Example

The images are reflected in a vertical mirror line. The correct answer is **E** and this has been marked on your answer sheet.

Now do the two practice questions below.

P1

In the completed pair, the larger (crescent) shape rotates 90° anti-clockwise while the smaller (triangle) shape rotates 90° clockwise. Applying the same changes to the first shape of the second pair means that **D** is the correct answer. Mark this answer in Practice Question 1 for Section 1 on your answer sheet.

P2

In the completed pair, the second shape is a reflection of the first shape in a vertical mirror line. Applying the same change to the first shape of the second pair means that **C** is the correct answer. Mark this answer in Practice Question 2 for Section 1 on your answer sheet.

You now have 6 minutes to complete the next 12 questions.

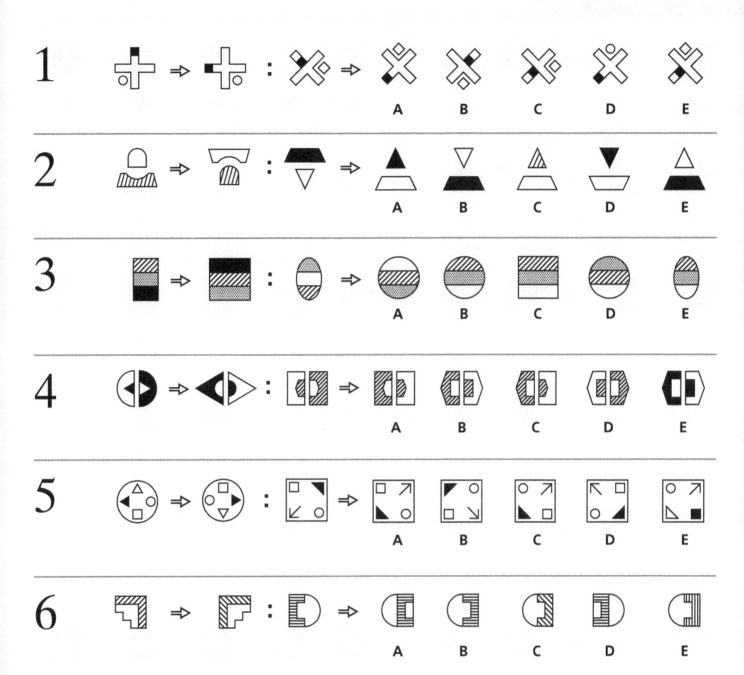

7 ⇒ : ⇒   ◯

                                           A   B   C   D   E

8 ⇒ : ... ⇒ ...

                                             A   B   C   D   E

9 ... ⇒ ... : ... ⇒ ...

                                             A   B   C   D   E

10 ... ⇒ ... : ... ⇒ ...

                                             A   B   C   D   E

11 ... ⇒ ... : ... ⇒ ...

                                             A   B   C   D   E

12 ... ⇒ ... : ... ⇒ ...

                                             A   B   C   D   E

Section 2

In the example below are five boxes arranged in order. One of the boxes is empty. One of the five boxes on the right should take the place of the empty one. Decide which one.

Example

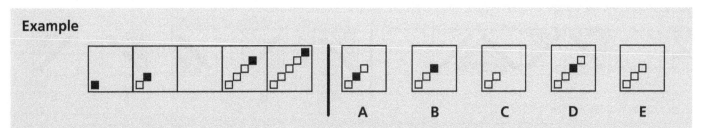

Looking at the boxes from left to right, the number of squares increases by one each time. The new square, added at the end of the pattern, is shaded black; the previous square becomes white. The correct answer is **B** and this has been marked on your answer sheet.

Now do the two practice questions below.

___

P1

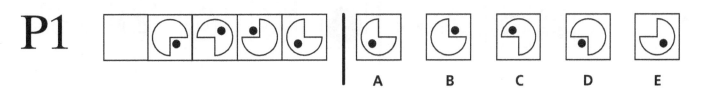

From left to right in this sequence, the circle moves up, left, down, etc. in an anti-clockwise direction, while the 'white' shape rotates 90° in a clockwise direction. We are looking for the first shape of the sequence, so the circle must be in the bottom left position and the 'white' shape must be 90° anti-clockwise to its position in the second box. So the correct answer is **A**. Mark this answer in Practice Question 1 for Section 2 on your answer sheet.

___

P2

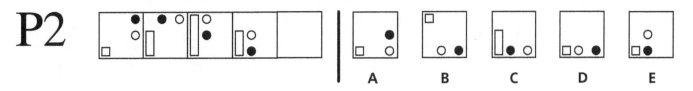

From left to right in this sequence, the circles move in an anti-clockwise direction while the square extends upwards into a rectangle, then further into a longer rectangle, before reducing to the previous rectangle size. We are looking for the last part of the sequence, so the circles will move to the next anti-clockwise position while the rectangle will reduce to a square size in the bottom left of the box. So the correct answer is **D**. Mark this answer in Practice Question 2 for Section 2 on your answer sheet.

___

You now have 6 minutes to complete the next 12 questions.

1

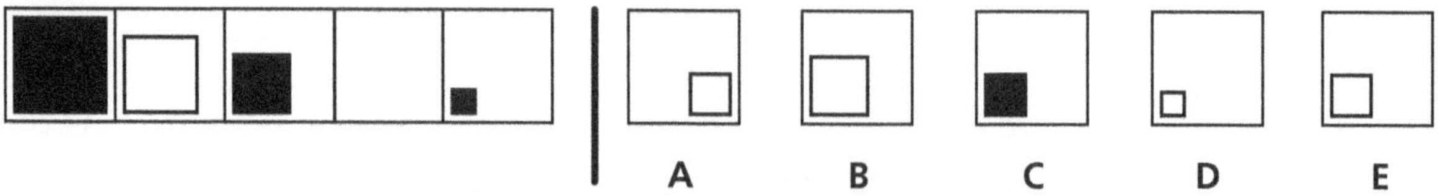

A   B   C   D   E

2

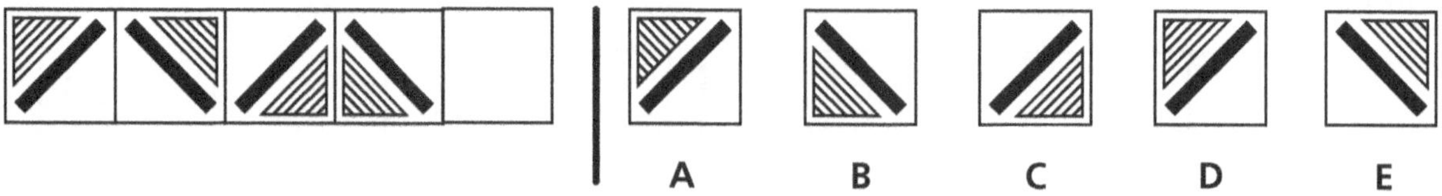

A   B   C   D   E

3

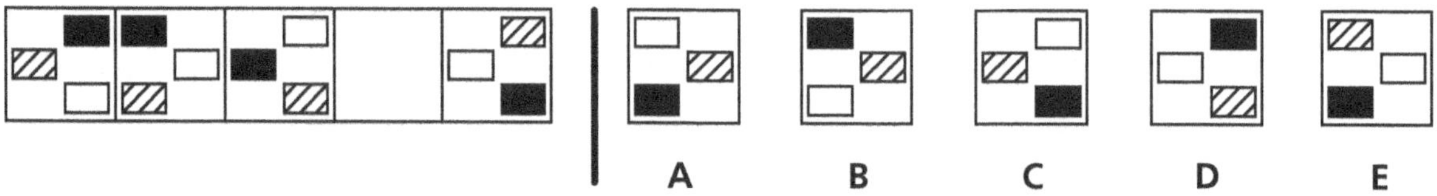

A   B   C   D   E

4

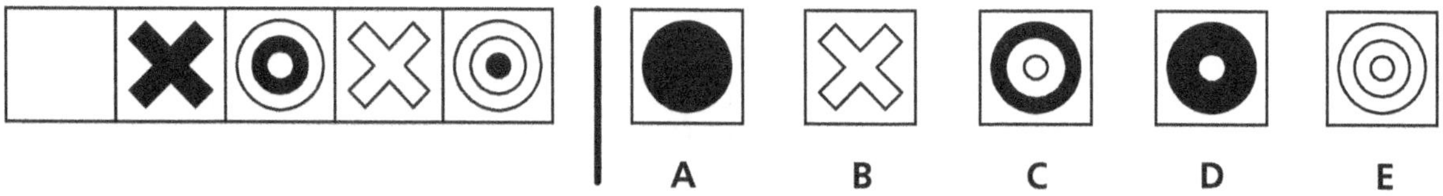

A   B   C   D   E

5

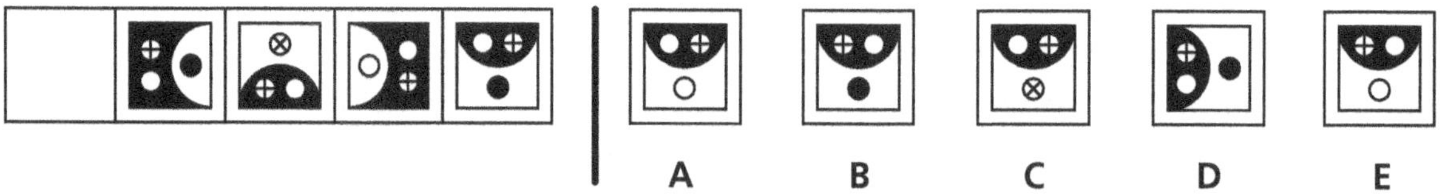

A   B   C   D   E

6

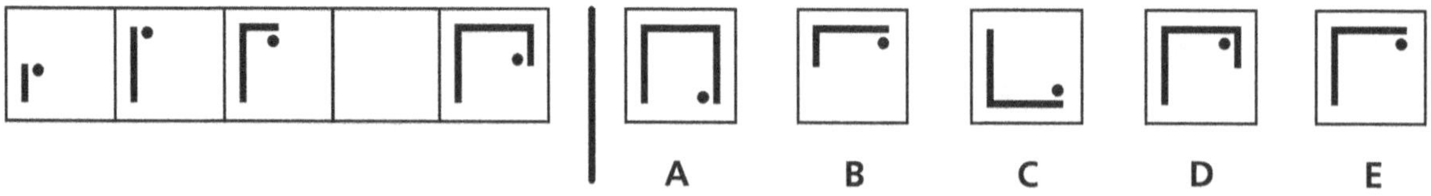

A   B   C   D   E

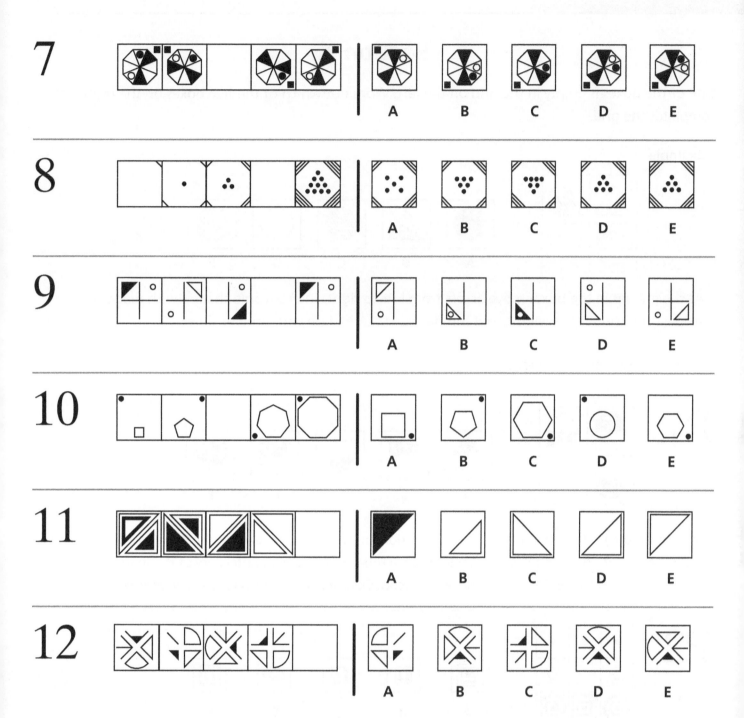

Section 3

One of the boxes is empty in the grid on the left. Work out which of the five boxes on the right completes the grid.

Example

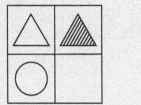

A   B   C   D   E

As the images in the boxes move across from left to right, they become shaded with diagonal stripes. The correct answer is **C** and this has been marked on your answer sheet.

Now do the two practice questions below.

P1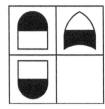

A   B   C   D   E

The shape in the bottom left of the grid is a reflection (in a horizontal line) of that in the top left, so we can expect the missing shape in the bottom right to be a reflection (in a horizontal line) of the shape top right. The answer is therefore **B**. Mark this answer in Practice Question 1 for Section 3 on your answer sheet.

P2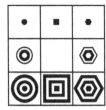

A   B   C   D   E

In each row, the pattern remains the same and in each column the shape remains in the same orientation. From left to right, the shape changes from circle to square to hexagon. In the centre of the middle row, we are therefore looking for a square shape positioned in the same way as the first and third rows and with a shading pattern to match the shapes in the second row, i.e. a white centre, followed by a black band, followed by a white band of the same width, followed by a thinner black outline. The correct answer is therefore **B**. Mark this answer in Practice Question 2 for Section 3 on your answer sheet.

> **You now have 6 minutes to complete the next 12 questions.**

1

A   B   C   D   E

2

A   B   C   D   E

3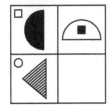

A   B   C   D   E

4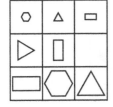

A   B   C   D   E

5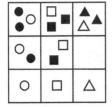

A   B   C   D   E

6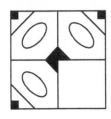

A   B   C   D   E

7 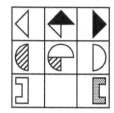 A B C D E

8 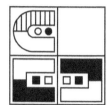 A B C D E

9 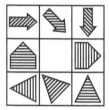 A B C D E

10 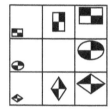 A B C D E

11 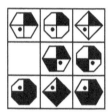 A B C D E

12 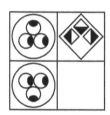 A B C D E

Section 4

Work out what makes the two images on the left similar to each other. Then find the image on the right that is **most like** the two images on the left.

Example

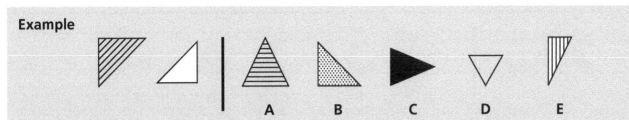

The two images on the left are right-angled triangles with two sides of equal length. Shape **B** is the only other right-angled triangle that has two sides of equal length. This has been marked on your answer sheet.

Now do the two practice questions below.

P1

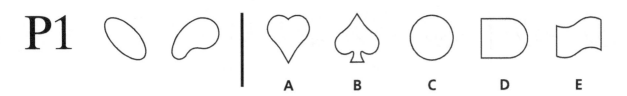

The two images on the left have no straight lines. Therefore the answer is the image on the right that has no straight lines, option **C**. Mark this answer in Practice Question 1 for Section 4 on your answer sheet.

P2

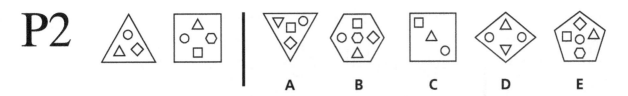

The number of small shapes within both images on the left matches the number of sides of the larger shape they are contained within, i.e. three within the triangle and four within the square. In addition, the small interior shapes are all different. Option **E** is therefore the correct answer as it has five different small shapes inside a pentagon. Mark this answer in Practice Question 2 for Section 4 on your answer sheet.

You now have 6 minutes to complete the next 12 questions.

1  |

A   B   C   D   E

2 |

A   B   C   D   E

3 |

A   B   C   D   E

4 |

A   B   C   D   E

5 |

A   B   C   D   E

6 |

A   B   C   D   E

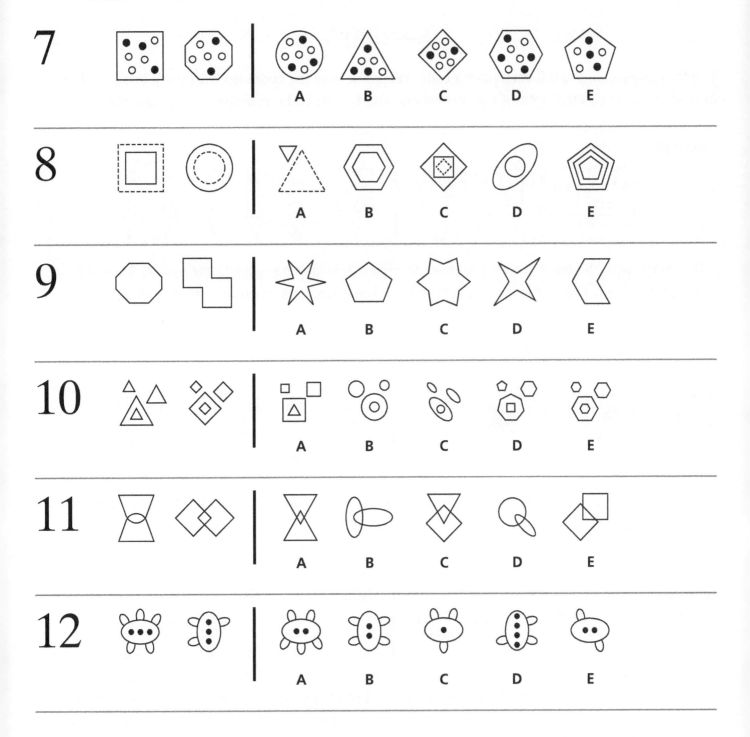

Section 5

The four images on the left each have a code. Work out how the codes go with these images. Then look at the image to the right of the vertical line and find its code from the five options given.

Example

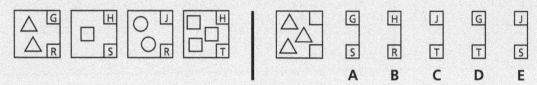

A   B   C   D   E

The image with the missing code has three triangles. Triangles have the letter code G. Three has the letter code T. The correct answer is **D** and this has been marked on your answer sheet.

Now do the two practice questions below.

P1

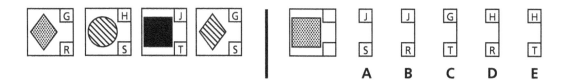

A   B   C   D   E

The image with the missing code has dots within a square. Looking at the first row of images, J is the code for a square and R is the code for dots, so the correct answer is **B**. Mark this answer in Practice Question 1 for Section 5 on your answer sheet.

P2

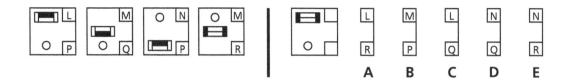

A   B   C   D   E

The image with the missing code shows a block positioned at the top with black-shaded ends. Looking at the first row of images, L is the code for the block in the top position and R is the code for the block style with black-shaded ends. The circle has no associated code. The correct answer is therefore **A**. Mark this answer in Practice Question 2 for Section 5 on your answer sheet.

> **You now have 6 minutes to complete the next 12 questions.**

1

2

3

4

5

6

A   B   C   D   E

7

H	J	K	J	H
Y	Z	Y	X	Z
A	**B**	**C**	**D**	**E**

8

L	N	M	N	L
Y	Z	X	Y	Z
A	**B**	**C**	**D**	**E**

9

T	S	R	S	T
Y	X	Z	Z	X
A	**B**	**C**	**D**	**E**

10

P	P	Q	R	R
M	N	L	N	M
A	**B**	**C**	**D**	**E**

11

Y	X	Y	X	W
K	K	L	M	M
A	**B**	**C**	**D**	**E**

12

J	G	H	J	G
L	M	N	M	N
A	**B**	**C**	**D**	**E**

END OF PAPER

Collins

Non-Verbal Reasoning Multiple Choice Practice Paper 2

Read these instructions carefully:

1. You must not open or turn over this booklet until you are told to do so.

2. The booklet contains a multiple-choice test, in which you have to mark your answer to each question on the separate answer sheet.

3. There are five sections in this test. Each section starts with an explanation of what to do, followed by an example. You will then be asked to do some practice questions. Explanations of the answers for these are included.

4. You should indicate one answer only for each question by drawing a firm pencil line clearly through the rectangle next to your answer on the answer sheet. Rub out any mistakes as well as you can and put in your new answer.

5. Complete the questions as quickly and as carefully as you can. If you find that you cannot do a question, do not waste time on it but go on to the next one.

6. You have 6 minutes to complete the 12 questions in each section.

7. You should do any rough working on a separate sheet of paper.

Section 1

Look at the line of five images. Work out which image is **most unlike** the other four.

Example

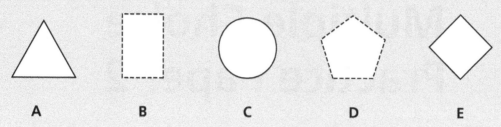

Shapes A, B, D and E all have straight sides; shape C is the only curved shape. The shape most unlike the others is **C** and this has been marked on your answer sheet.

Now do the two practice questions below.

P1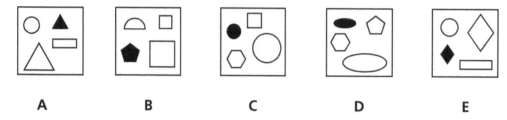

In four of the five images, the black-shaded shape is a smaller version of the largest shape within the same set. The only option where this is not the case is B. So **B** is most unlike the others. Mark this answer in Practice Question 1 for Section 1 on your answer sheet.

P2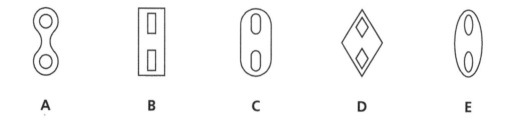

In four of the five images, a large shape encloses a smaller pair of the same shape. The only option where this is not the case is A, where we would have expected a full circle to enclose the two smaller ones. So **A** is most unlike the others. Mark this answer in Practice Question 2 for Section 1 on your answer sheet.

> **You now have 6 minutes to complete the next 12 questions.**

1

A   B   C   D   E

2

A   B   C   D   E

3

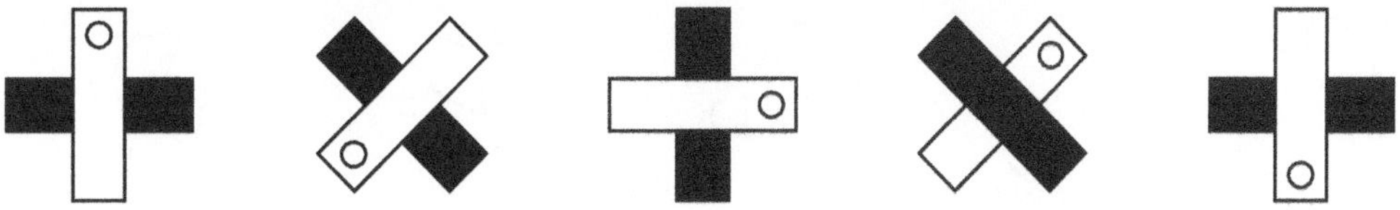

A   B   C   D   E

4

A   B   C   D   E

5

A   B   C   D   E

6

A   B   C   D   E

7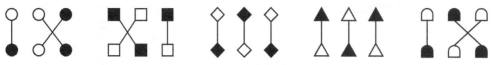

    A   B   C   D   E

8

    A   B   C   D   E

9

    A   B   C   D   E

10

    A   B   C   D   E

11

    A   B   C   D   E

12

    A   B   C   D   E

Section 2

Look at the given net on the left. Work out which one of the cubes on the right can be made using that net.

Example

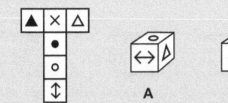

The double-headed arrow will point to the cross and the white circle. The triangle will point to the double-headed arrow. Therefore the answer is **C** and this has been marked on your answer sheet.

Now do the two practice questions below.

P1

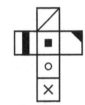   

A   B   C   D   E

If the circle is at the top of the cube, the cross will be on the front face and the triangle to its right. **E** is therefore the correct answer. Mark this answer in Practice Question 1 for Section 2 on your answer sheet.

P2

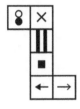

A   B   C   D   E

If the arrow with a black head is pointing upwards on the front face, it will be pointing towards the white circle on the top face of the cube and the black square will be on the face to the right of the arrow. Therefore the answer is **A**. Mark this answer in Practice Question 2 for Section 2 on your answer sheet.

> **You now have 6 minutes to complete the next 12 questions.**

1

   A   B   C   D   E

2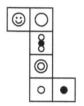

   A   B   C   D   E

3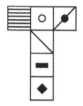

   A   B   C   D   E

4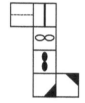

   A   B   C   D   E

5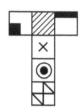

   A   B   C   D   E

6

   A   B   C   D   E

7

A   B   C   D   E

8

A   B   C   D   E

9

A   B   C   D   E

10

A   B   C   D   E

11

A   B   C   D   E

12

A   B   C   D   E

Section 3

In the example below are two images on the left with an arrow between them. Then there is a third image with an arrow pointing to five more images. Decide which one of these five images goes with the third image to make a pair like the two on the left.

Example

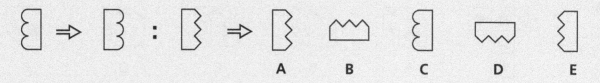

The images are reflected in a vertical mirror line. The correct answer is **E** and this has been marked on your answer sheet.

Now do the two practice questions below.

P1

In the completed pair, the larger (crescent) shape rotates 90° anti-clockwise while the smaller (triangle) shape rotates 90° clockwise. Applying the same changes to the first shape of the second pair means that **D** is the correct answer. Mark this answer in Practice Question 1 for Section 3 on your answer sheet.

P2

In the completed pair, the second shape is a reflection of the first shape in a vertical mirror line. Applying the same change to the first shape of the second pair means that **C** is the correct answer. Mark this answer in Practice Question 2 for Section 3 on your answer sheet.

You now have 6 minutes to complete the next 12 questions.

1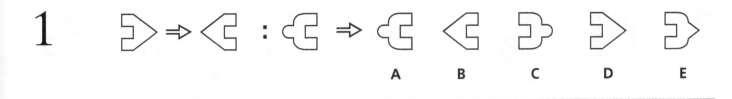

2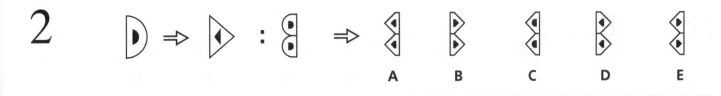

3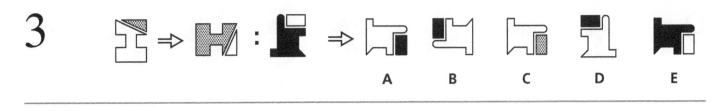

4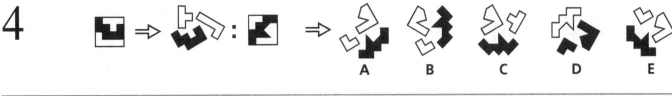

5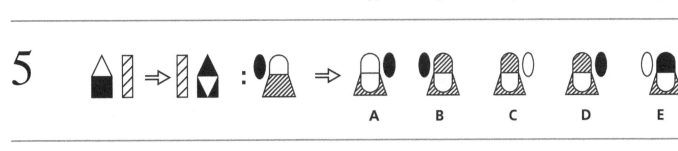

6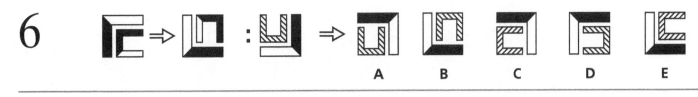

7 → : ⇒

A   B   C   D   E

8 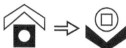 : ⇒

A   B   C   D   E

9 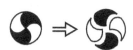 : ⇒

A   B   C   D   E

10 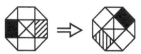 :   ⇒

A   B   C   D   E

11 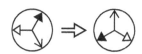 :   ⇒

A   B   C   D   E

12  :   ⇒

A   B   C   D   E

Section 4

In the example below are five boxes arranged in order. One of the boxes is empty. One of the five boxes on the right should take the place of the empty one. Decide which one.

Example

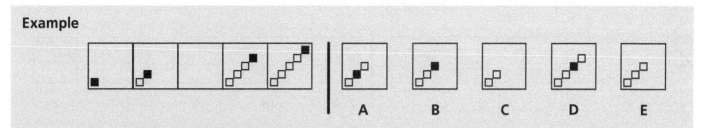

Looking at the boxes from left to right, the number of squares increases by one each time. The new square, added at the end of the pattern, is shaded black; the previous square becomes white. The correct answer is **B** and this has been marked on your answer sheet.

Now do the two practice questions below.

P1

From left to right in this sequence, the circle moves up, left, down, etc. in an anti-clockwise direction, while the 'white' shape rotates 90° in a clockwise direction. We are looking for the first shape of the sequence, so the circle must be in the bottom left position and the 'white' shape must be 90° anti-clockwise to its position in the second box. So the correct answer is **A**. Mark this answer in Practice Question 1 for Section 4 on your answer sheet.

P2
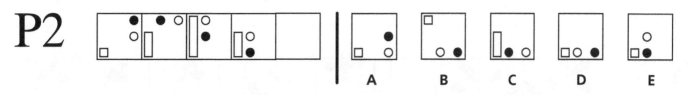

From left to right in this sequence, the circles move in an anti-clockwise direction while the square extends upwards into a rectangle, then further into a longer rectangle, before reducing to the previous rectangle size. We are looking for the last part of the sequence, so the circles will move to the next anti-clockwise position while the rectangle will reduce to a square size in the bottom left of the box. So the correct answer is **D**. Mark this answer in Practice Question 2 for Section 4 on your answer sheet.

> **You now have 6 minutes to complete the next 12 questions.**

1

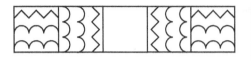

| A | B | C | D | E |

2

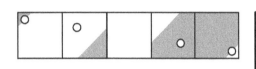

| A | B | C | D | E |

3

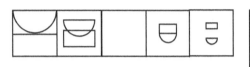

| A | B | C | D | E |

4

| A | B | C | D | E |

5

| A | B | C | D | E |

6

| A | B | C | D | E |

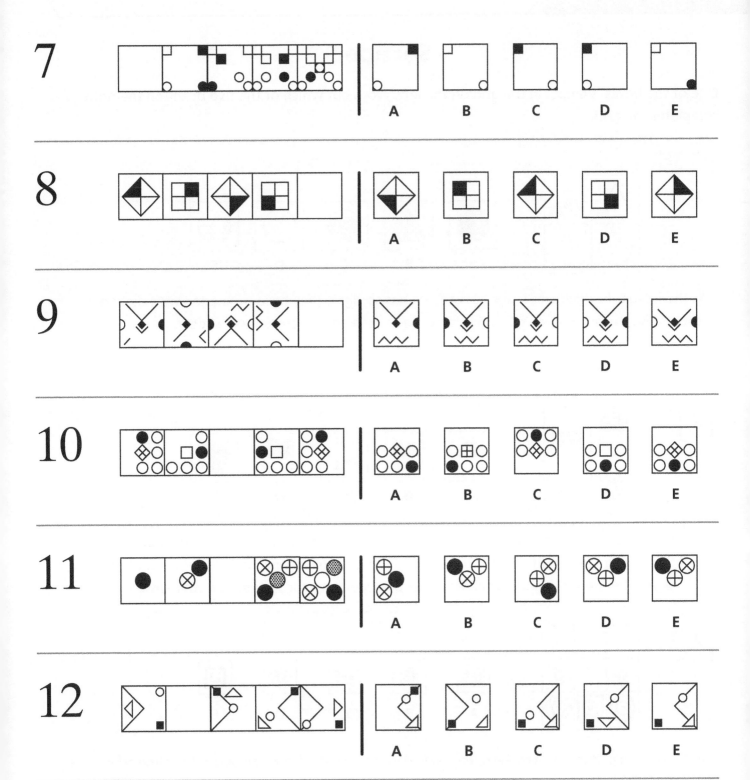

Section 5

One of the boxes is empty in the grid on the left. Work out which of the five boxes on the right completes the grid.

Example

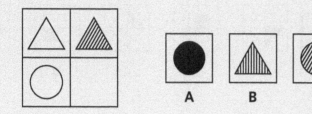

As the images in the boxes move across from left to right, they become shaded with diagonal stripes. The correct answer is **C** and this has been marked on your answer sheet.

Now do the two practice questions below.

P1

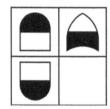

The shape in the bottom left of the grid is a reflection (in a horizontal line) of that in the top left, so we can expect the missing shape in the bottom right to be a reflection (in a horizontal line) of the shape top right. The answer is therefore **B**. Mark this answer in Practice Question 1 for Section 5 on your answer sheet.

P2

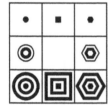

In each row, the pattern remains the same and in each column the shape remains in the same orientation. From left to right, the shape changes from circle to square to hexagon. In the centre of the middle row, we are therefore looking for a square shape positioned in the same way as the first and third rows and with a shading pattern to match the shapes in the second row, i.e. a white centre, followed by a black band, followed by a white band of the same width, followed by a thinner black outline. The correct answer is therefore **B**. Mark this answer in Practice Question 2 for Section 5 on your answer sheet.

> ### You now have 6 minutes to complete the next 12 questions.

1

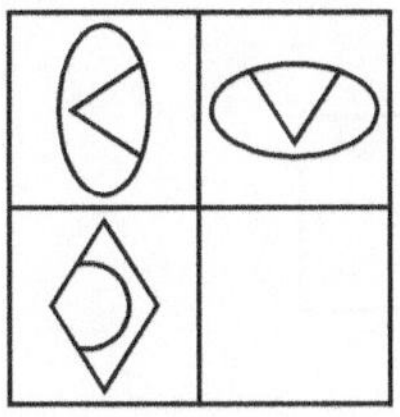

A B C D E

2

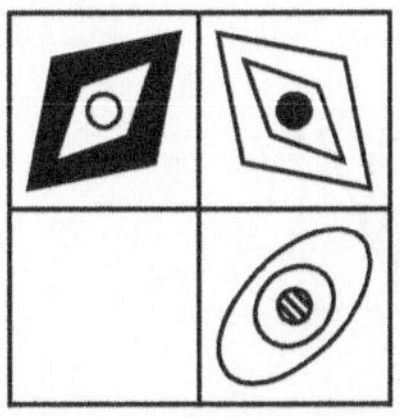

A B C D E

3

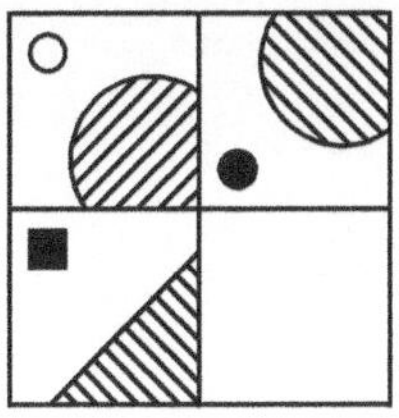

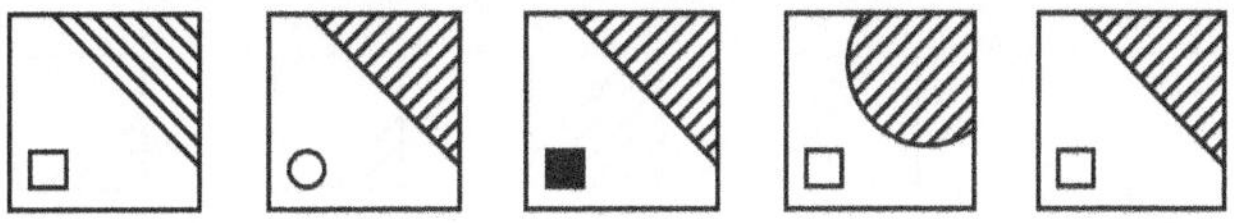

A B C D E

4

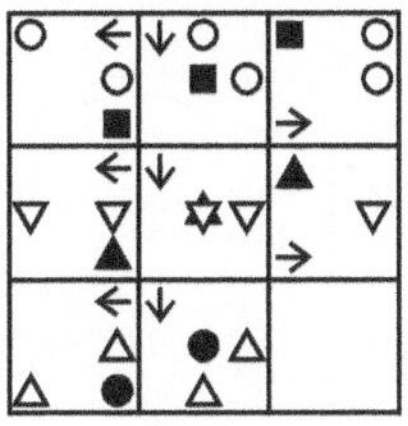

A B C D E

5

A B C D E

6

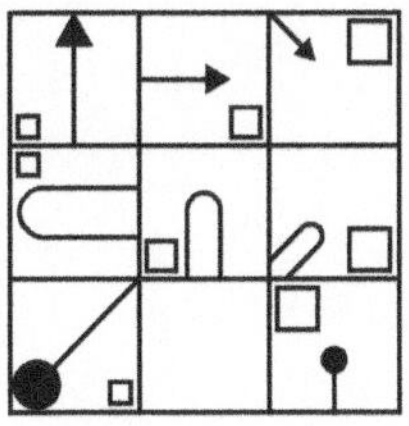

A B C D E

7

A B C D E

8

A   B   C   D   E

9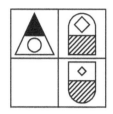

A   B   C   D   E

10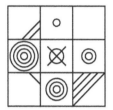

A   B   C   D   E

11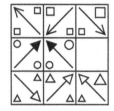

A   B   C   D   E

12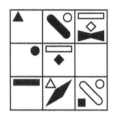

A   B   C   D   E

END OF PAPER

Collins

Non-Verbal Reasoning Multiple Choice Practice Paper 3

Read these instructions carefully:

1. You must not open or turn over this booklet until you are told to do so.

2. The booklet contains a multiple-choice test, in which you have to mark your answer to each question on the separate answer sheet.

3. There are five sections in this test. Each section starts with an explanation of what to do, followed by an example. You will then be asked to do some practice questions. Explanations of the answers for these are included.

4. You should indicate one answer only for each question by drawing a firm pencil line clearly through the rectangle next to your answer on the answer sheet. Rub out any mistakes as well as you can and put in your new answer.

5. Complete the questions as quickly and as carefully as you can. If you find that you cannot do a question, do not waste time on it but go on to the next one.

6. You have 6 minutes to complete the 12 questions in each section.

7. You should do any rough working on a separate sheet of paper.

Section 1

Work out what makes the two images on the left similar to each other. Then find the image on the right that is **most like** the two images on the left.

Example

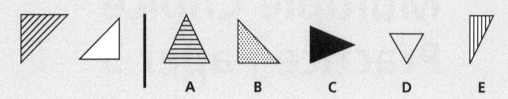

The two images on the left are right-angled triangles with two sides of equal length. Shape **B** is the only other right-angled triangle that has two sides of equal length. This has been marked on your answer sheet.

Now do the two practice questions below.

P1

A   B   C   D   E

The two images on the left have no straight lines. Therefore the answer is the image on the right that has no straight lines, option **C**. Mark this answer in Practice Question 1 for Section 1 on your answer sheet.

P2

A   B   C   D   E

The number of small shapes within both images on the left matches the number of sides of the larger shape they are contained within, i.e. three within the triangle and four within the square. In addition, the small interior shapes are all different. Option **E** is therefore the correct answer as it has five different small shapes inside a pentagon. Mark this answer in Practice Question 2 for Section 1 on your answer sheet.

You now have 6 minutes to complete the next 12 questions.

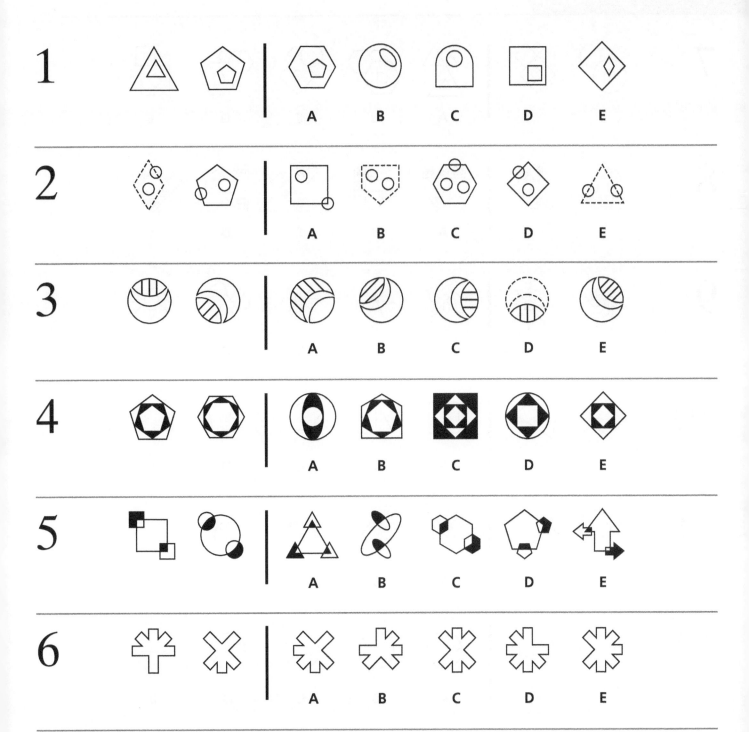

1

2

3

4

5

6

A   B   C   D   E

7 |

A   B   C   D   E

8 |

A   B   C   D   E

9 |

A   B   C   D   E

10 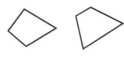 |

A   B   C   D   E

11 |

A   B   C   D   E

12 |

A   B   C   D   E

Section 2

The four images on the left each have a code. Work out how the codes go with these images. Then look at the image to the right of the vertical line and find its code from the five options given.

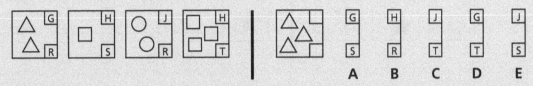
Now do the two practice questions below.

P1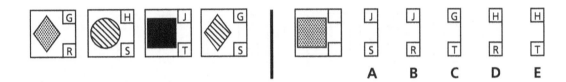

The image with the missing code has dots within a square. Looking at the first row of images, J is the code for a square and R is the code for dots, so the correct answer is **B**. Mark this answer in Practice Question 1 for Section 2 on your answer sheet.

P2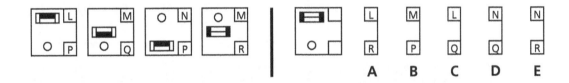

The image with the missing code shows a block positioned at the top with black-shaded ends. Looking at the first row of images, L is the code for the block in the top position and R is the code for the block style with black-shaded ends. The circle has no associated code. The correct answer is therefore **A**. Mark this answer in Practice Question 2 for Section 2 on your answer sheet.

You now have 6 minutes to complete the next 12 questions.

1

   |

T	S	T	T	S
Y	Y	X	Z	Z
A	B	C	D	E

2

   |

R	T	R	T	R
Z	X	X	Z	Y
A	B	C	D	E

3

    |

P	P	R	Q	R
X	W	V	X	W
A	B	C	D	E

4

   |

Y	Y	Z	Y	Z
G	F	H	H	F
A	B	C	D	E

5

    |

T	T	R	S	Q
K	J	L	K	L
A	B	C	D	E

6

   |

R	S	S	R	S
G	H	F	H	G
A	B	C	D	E

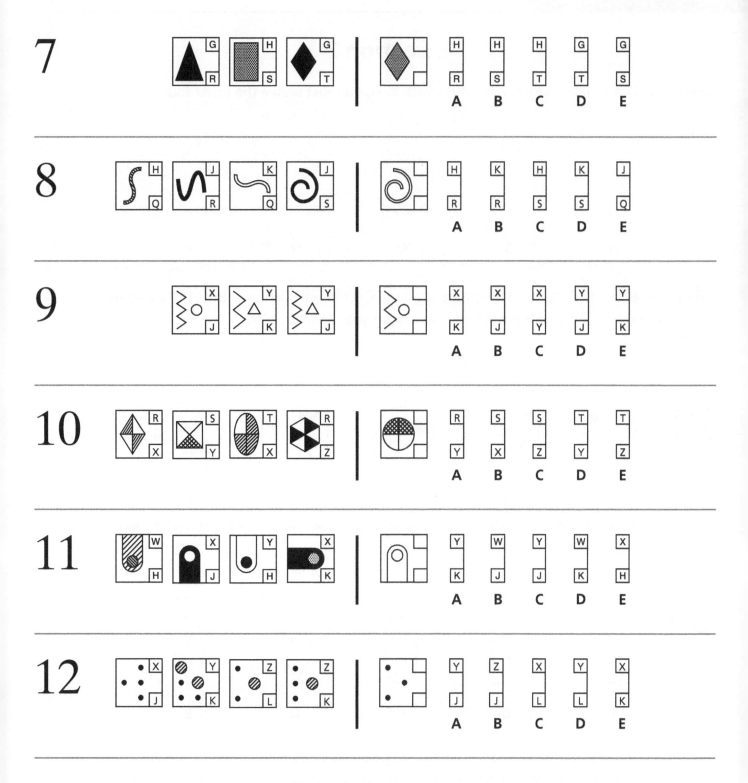

Section 3

Look at the line of five images. Work out which image is **most unlike** the other four.

Example

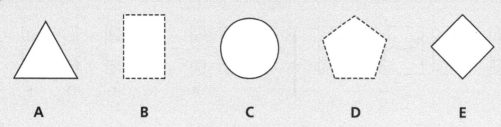

A   B   C   D   E

Shapes A, B, D and E all have straight sides; shape C is the only curved shape. The shape most unlike the others is **C** and this has been marked on your answer sheet.

Now do the two practice questions below.

P1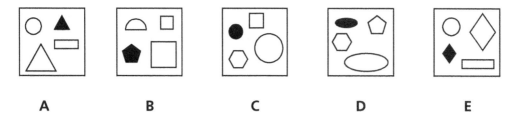

A   B   C   D   E

In four of the five images, the black-shaded shape is a smaller version of the largest shape within the same set. The only option where this is not the case is B. So **B** is most unlike the others. Mark this answer in Practice Question 1 for Section 3 on your answer sheet.

P2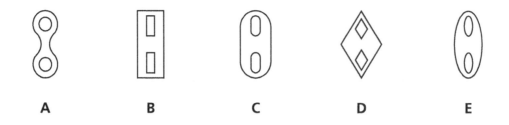

A   B   C   D   E

In four of the five images, a large shape encloses a smaller pair of the same shape. The only option where this is not the case is A, where we would have expected a full circle to enclose the two smaller ones. So **A** is most unlike the others. Mark this answer in Practice Question 2 for Section 3 on your answer sheet.

You now have 6 minutes to complete the next 12 questions.

1

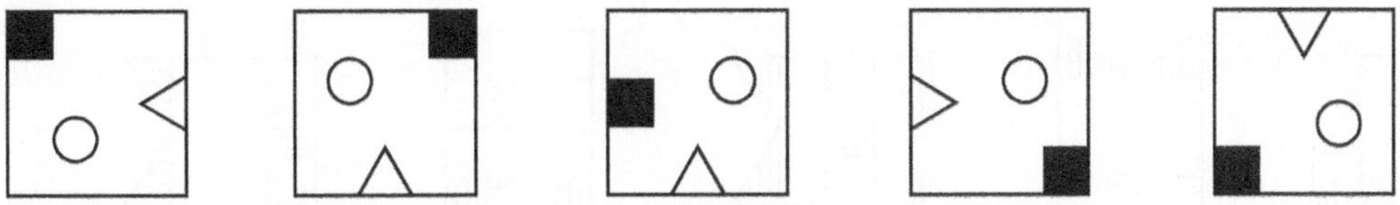

A B C D E

2

A B C D E

3

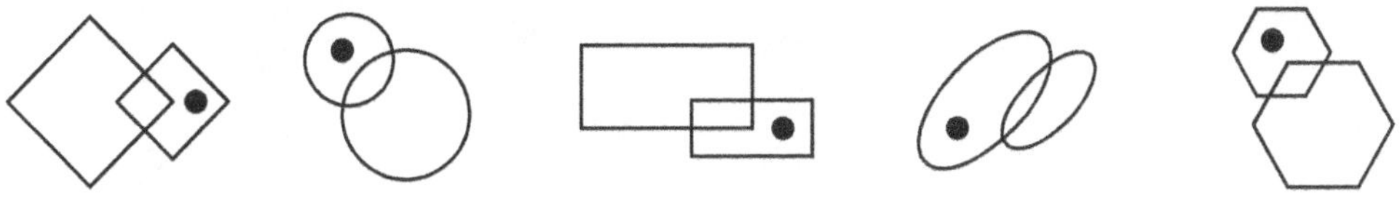

A B C D E

4

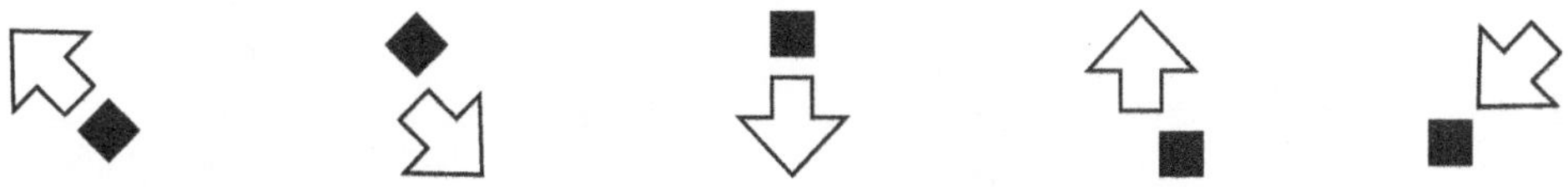

A B C D E

5

A B C D E

6

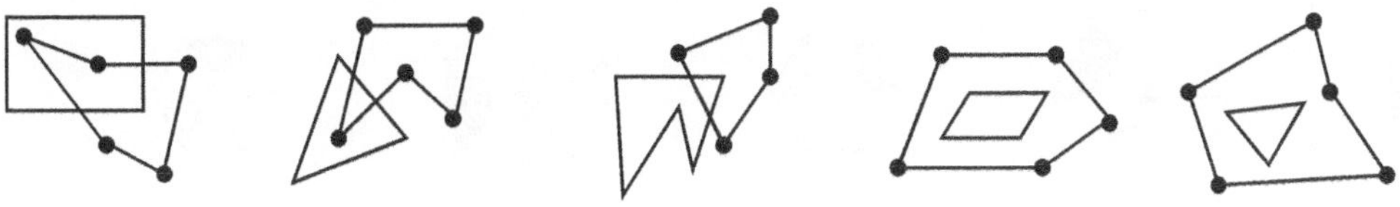

A B C D E

7

    A   B   C   D   E

8

    A   B   C   D   E

9

    A   B   C   D   E

10

    A   B   C   D   E

11

    A   B   C   D   E

12

    A   B   C   D   E

Section 4

Look at the given 3D figure. Work out which one of the five options shows the top-down (plan) view of that figure.

Example

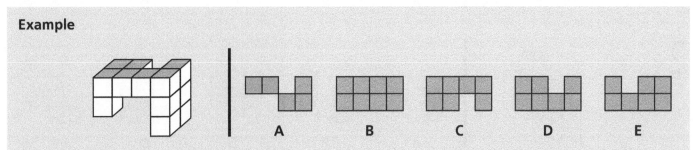

The figure shows four cubes in the front row and three cubes in the back row with a gap in the second column from the right-hand side. The answer is therefore **D** and this has been marked on your answer sheet.

Now do the two practice questions below.

P1

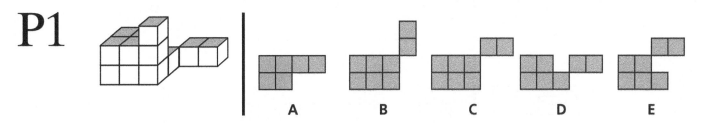

The figure has three cubes in the front row, three cubes in the second row and two cubes in the third row, attached at the corner. The correct answer is therefore **C**. Mark this answer in Practice Question 1 for Section 4 on your answer sheet.

P2

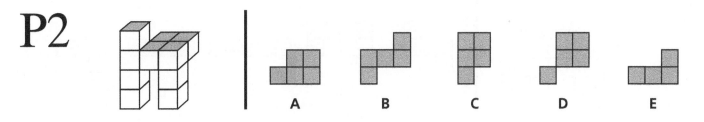

The figure has three cubes in the first row and two cubes in the second row aligned with the right-hand side of the figure. The correct answer is therefore **A**. Mark this answer in Practice Question 2 for Section 4 on your answer sheet.

> **You now have 6 minutes to complete the next 12 questions.**

1 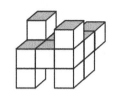 | A   B   C   D   E

2 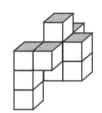 | 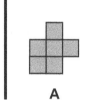 A   B   C   D   E

3 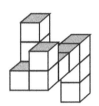 | 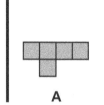 A 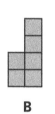 B 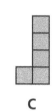 C 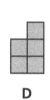 D   E

4 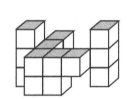 | A   B   C   D   E

5 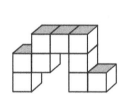 | A   B  C   D   E

6 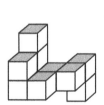 | A   B   C   D   E

7

| A | B | C | D | E |

8

| A | B | C | D | E |

9

| A | B | C | D | E |

10

| A | B | C | D | E |

11

| A | B | C | D | E |

12

| A | B | C | D | E |

Section 5

In the example below are two images on the left with an arrow between them. Then there is a third image with an arrow pointing to five more images. Decide which one of these five images goes with the third image to make a pair like the two on the left.

Example

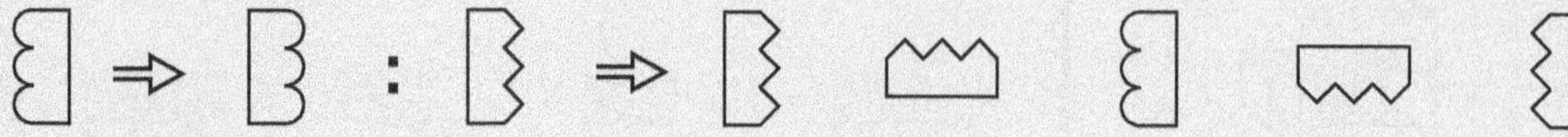

A   B   C   D   E

The images are reflected in a vertical mirror line. The correct answer is **E** and this has been marked on your answer sheet.

Now do the two practice questions below.

P1

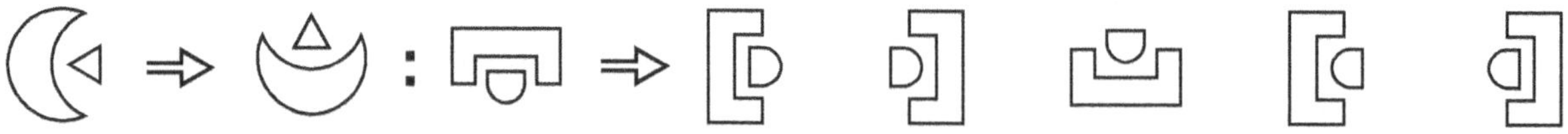

A   B   C   D   E

In the completed pair, the larger (crescent) shape rotates 90° anti-clockwise while the smaller (triangle) shape rotates 90° clockwise. Applying the same changes to the first shape of the second pair means that **D** is the correct answer. Mark this answer in Practice Question 1 for Section 5 on your answer sheet.

P2

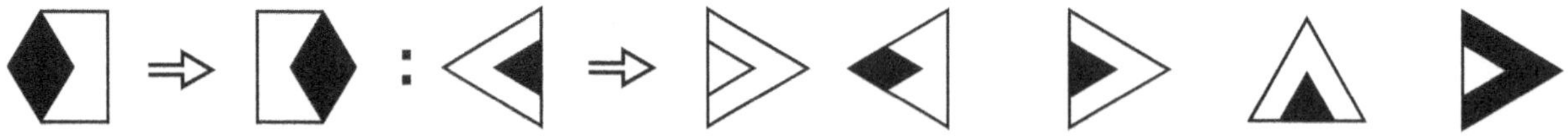

A   B   C   D   E

In the completed pair, the second shape is a reflection of the first shape in a vertical mirror line. Applying the same change to the first shape of the second pair means that **C** is the correct answer. Mark this answer in Practice Question 2 for Section 5 on your answer sheet.

> **You now have 6 minutes to complete the next 12 questions.**

1

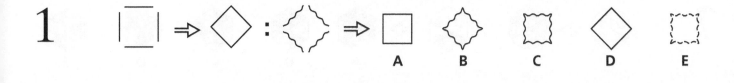

2

3

4

5

6

7 ⇒ : ⇒

                                                               A   B   C   D   E

8 :  ⇒

                                                               A   B   C   D   E

9  : ⇒

                                                               A   B   C   D   E

10  : ⇒

                                                               A   B   C   D   E

11  ⇒

                                                               A   B   C   D   E

12 (image) : (image) ⇒ (A) (B) (C) (D) (E)

                                                               A   B   C   D   E

END OF PAPER

Collins

Non-Verbal Reasoning Multiple Choice Practice Paper 4

Read these instructions carefully:

1. You must not open or turn over this booklet until you are told to do so.

2. The booklet contains a multiple-choice test, in which you have to mark your answer to each question on the separate answer sheet.

3. There are five sections in this test. Each section starts with an explanation of what to do, followed by an example. You will then be asked to do some practice questions. Explanations of the answers for these are included.

4. You should indicate one answer only for each question by drawing a firm pencil line clearly through the rectangle next to your answer on the answer sheet. Rub out any mistakes as well as you can and put in your new answer.

5. Complete the questions as quickly and as carefully as you can. If you find that you cannot do a question, do not waste time on it but go on to the next one.

6. You have 6 minutes to complete the 12 questions in each section.

7. You should do any rough working on a separate sheet of paper.

Section 1

In the example below are five boxes arranged in order. One of the boxes is empty. One of the five boxes on the right should take the place of the empty one. Decide which one.

Example

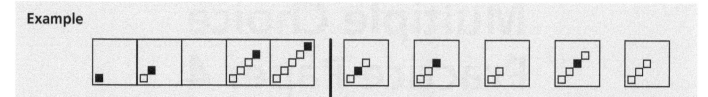

Looking at the boxes from left to right, the number of squares increases by one each time. The new square, added at the end of the pattern, is shaded black; the previous square becomes white. The correct answer is **B** and this has been marked on your answer sheet.

Now do the two practice questions below.

P1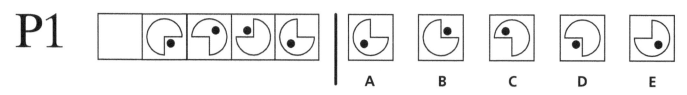

From left to right in this sequence, the circle moves up, left, down, etc. in an anti-clockwise direction, while the 'white' shape rotates 90° in a clockwise direction. We are looking for the first shape of the sequence, so the circle must be in the bottom left position and the 'white' shape must be 90° anti-clockwise to its position in the second box. So the correct answer is **A**. Mark this answer in Practice Question 1 for Section 1 on your answer sheet.

P2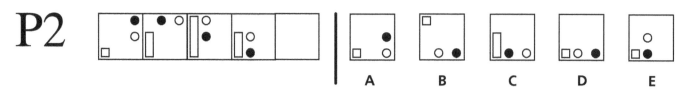

From left to right in this sequence, the circles move in an anti-clockwise direction while the square extends upwards into a rectangle, then further into a longer rectangle, before reducing to the previous rectangle size. We are looking for the last part of the sequence, so the circles will move to the next anti-clockwise position while the rectangle will reduce to a square size in the bottom left of the box. So the correct answer is **D**. Mark this answer in Practice Question 2 for Section 1 on your answer sheet.

You now have 6 minutes to complete the next 12 questions.

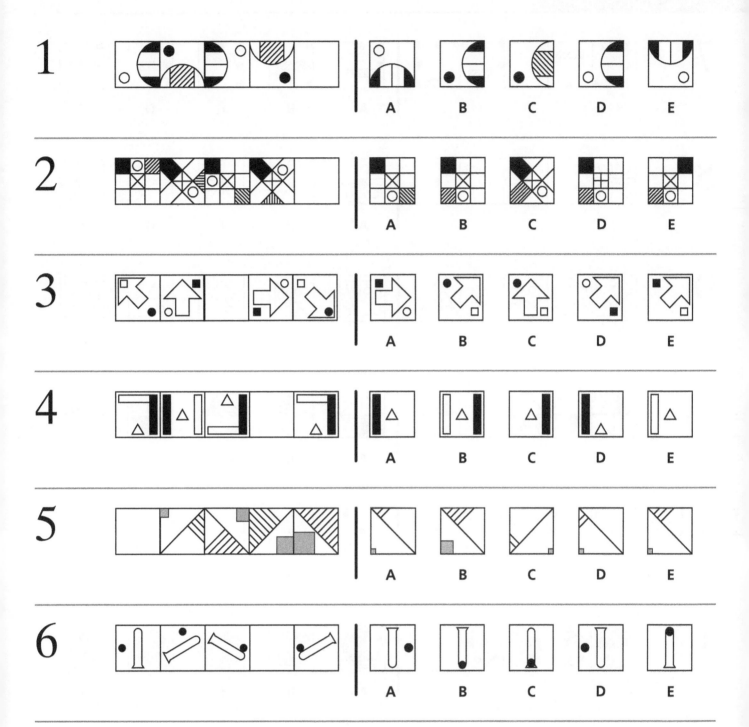

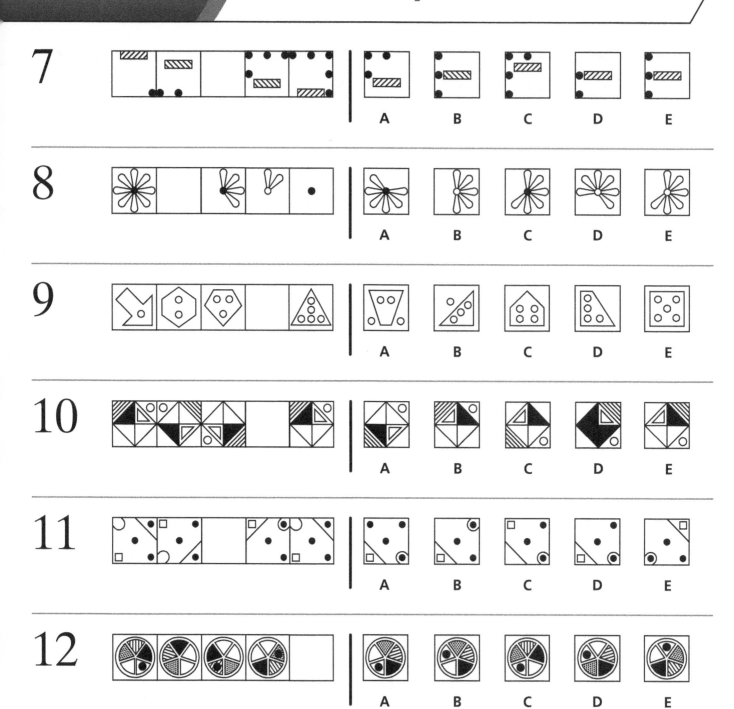

Section 2

One of the boxes is empty in the grid on the left. Work out which of the five boxes on the right completes the grid.

Example

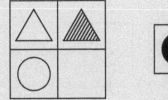 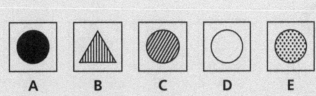

As the images in the boxes move across from left to right, they become shaded with diagonal stripes. The correct answer is **C** and this has been marked on your answer sheet.

Now do the two practice questions below.

P1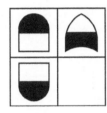

                                  A   B   C   D   E

The shape in the bottom left of the grid is a reflection (in a horizontal line) of that in the top left, so we can expect the missing shape in the bottom right to be a reflection (in a horizontal line) of the shape top right. The answer is therefore **B**. Mark this answer in Practice Question 1 for Section 2 on your answer sheet.

P2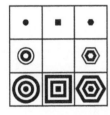

                                  A   B   C   D   E

In each row, the pattern remains the same and in each column the shape remains in the same orientation. From left to right, the shape changes from circle to square to hexagon. In the centre of the middle row, we are therefore looking for a square shape positioned in the same way as the first and third rows and with a shading pattern to match the shapes in the second row, i.e. a white centre, followed by a black band, followed by a white band of the same width, followed by a thinner black outline. The correct answer is therefore **B**. Mark this answer in Practice Question 2 for Section 2 on your answer sheet.

> **You now have 6 minutes to complete the next 12 questions.**

1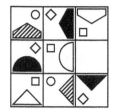

    A   B   C   D   E

2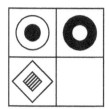

    A   B   C   D   E

3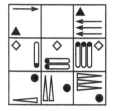

    A   B   C   D   E

4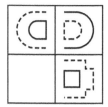

    A   B   C   D   E

5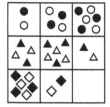

    A   B   C   D   E

6

    A   B   C   D   E

7

A **B** **C** **D** **E**

8

A **B** **C** **D** **E**

9

A **B** **C** **D** **E**

10

A **B** **C** **D** **E**

11

A **B** **C** **D** **E**

12

A **B** **C** **D** **E**

Section 3

Work out which shape or pattern from the right-hand side belongs to the set on the left-hand side.

Example

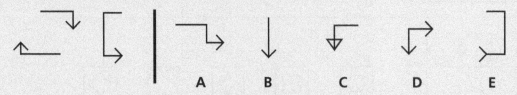

The images on the left each have the same style of arrowhead and have at least one bend in the arrow itself. B does not fit because it is a straight arrow, C does not fit because it has the wrong style of arrowhead, D has two arrowheads and in E the arrowhead is reversed.

The only option that completes the set is **A** and this has been marked on your answer sheet.

Now do the two practice questions below.

P1

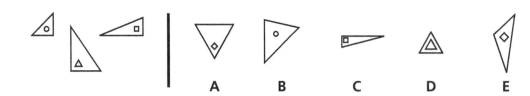

The three shapes on the left all consist of triangles with a smaller shape placed at the right angle. The only answer option matching this pattern is **C**. Mark this answer in Practice Question 1 for Section 3 on your answer sheet.

P2

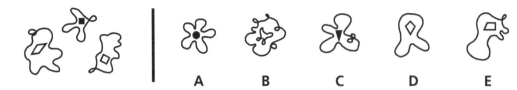

The three images on the left all contain a four-sided shape. The only common pattern between the loops is that they have one overlap. The only answer option with a four-sided shape within a loop that has one overlap is **E**. Mark this answer in Practice Question 2 for Section 3 on your answer sheet.

You now have 6 minutes to complete the next 12 questions.

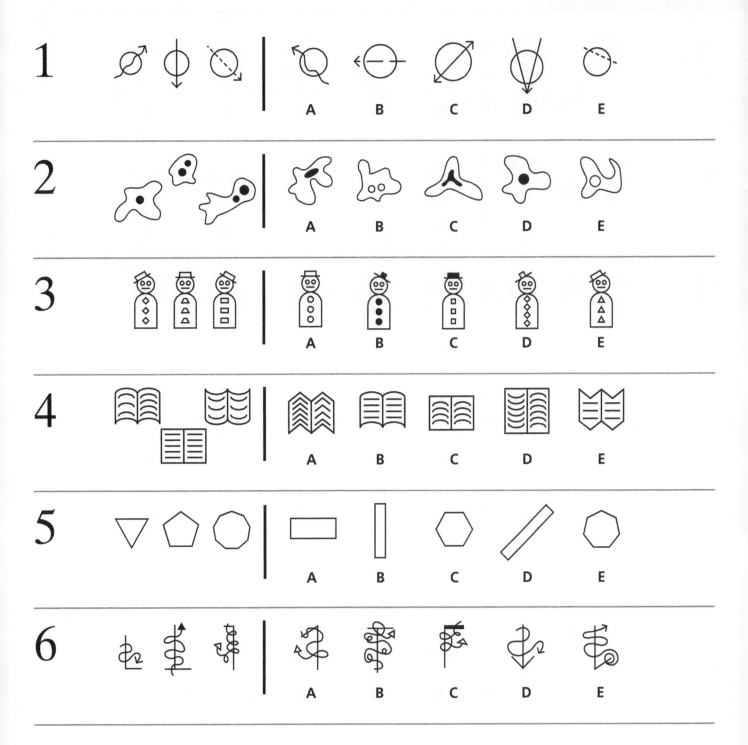

7 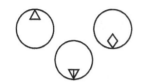 |

A   B   C   D   E

8

A   B   C   D   E

9  |

A   B   C   D   E

10  |

A   B   C   D   E

11 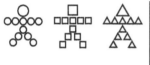 |

A   B   C   D   E

12  |

A   B   C   D   E

Section 4

The images on the left each have a code. Work out how the codes go with these images. Then look at the image to the right of the vertical line and find its code from the five options given.

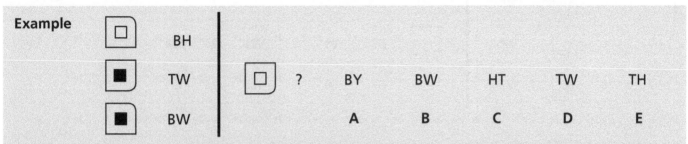

The two figures that start with the code 'B' both have a curved corner in the upper right of the outer square. The figure that starts with the code 'T' has a curved corner in the lower right of the outer square. So the code for the new figure must start with 'T'. The two figures that end with the code 'W' both have a black inner square. The figure that has a white inner square has the final letter 'H'. So the new figure must have a code that ends in 'H'. Therefore the correct answer is **E** and this has been marked on your answer sheet.

Now do the two practice questions below.

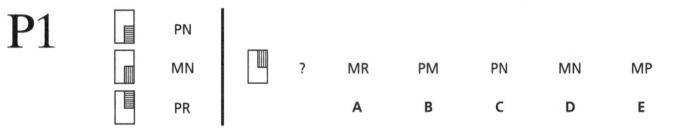

The two figures whose codes start with 'P' both have horizontal striped shading. The one starting with 'M' has vertical striped shading. The two figures whose codes end with 'N' have the inner rectangle in the bottom right-hand corner. The figure whose code ends with 'R' has the inner rectangle in the top right-hand corner. Therefore 'MR' is the correct code for the given figure and this is answer **A**. Mark this answer in Practice Question 1 for Section 4 on your answer sheet.

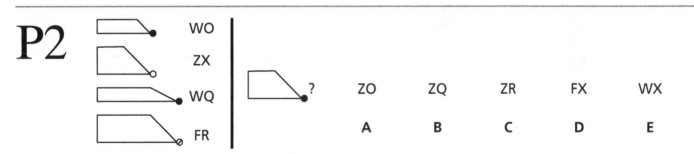

The two figures with codes starting with 'W' both have black circles. The figure with a code starting 'Z' has a white circle and the figure with a code starting 'F' has a circle with a diagonal stripe. Each figure has a different shaped trapezium corresponding to the second letter of the code. Therefore the figure on the right has the code 'WX' and this is answer **E**.

Mark this answer in Practice Question 2 for Section 4 on your answer sheet.

> You now have 6 minutes to complete the next 12 questions.

1  VI

VP

WZ

  ?

VI	WI	WP	VZ	WZ
A	**B**	**C**	**D**	**E**

2 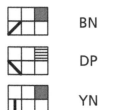 BN

DP

YN

BM

?

BP	DM	BN	YP	YM
A	**B**	**C**	**D**	**E**

3 SQE

 RWF

 SWG

?

SWF	RQE	RQF	SQF	SWE
A	**B**	**C**	**D**	**E**

4 QV

 QD

 EP

 EF

?

QF	ED	EV	QD	QP
A	**B**	**C**	**D**	**E**

5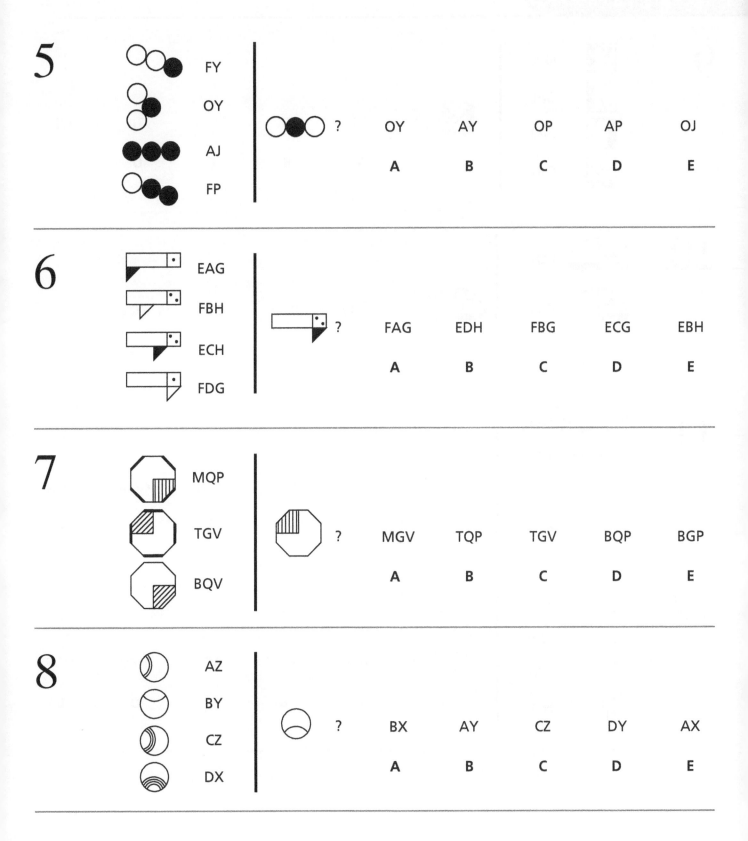

FY

OY

AJ

FP

? OY AY OP AP OJ

A B C D E

6

EAG

FBH

ECH

FDG

? FAG EDH FBG ECG EBH

A B C D E

7

MQP

TGV

BQV

? MGV TQP TGV BQP BGP

A B C D E

8

AZ

BY

CZ

DX

? BX AY CZ DY AX

A B C D E

9 FHK

 GHL

 GIM

 GJN

 ?

FIL	FJK	GHM	GJL	FJL
A	B	C	D	E

10 RQV

 ROY

 ZOV

?

RQV	RQY	ZQY	ZQV	ZOY
A	B	C	D	E

11 GTA

FPA

GOB

GZN

?

GZB	FZA	FTN	GOA	FON
A	B	C	D	E

12 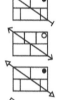 ACN

HDV

 ACW

HEF

?

ACF	HDW	AEV	HEV	HDF
A	B	C	D	E

Section 5

Look at the shape on the left. The shape is hidden in one of the five images on the right. Find which image contains the given shape.

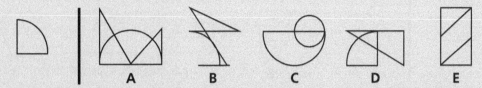
Now do the two practice questions below.

P1

        A   B   C   D   E

The hidden shape is a semi-circle. It only appears at this size in option **A**. Mark this answer in Practice Question 1 for Section 5 on your answer sheet.

P2   

        A   B   C   D   E

The hidden shape is an irregular pentagon. It only appears at this size in option **B**. Mark this answer in Practice Question 2 for Section 5 on your answer sheet.

You now have 6 minutes to complete the next 12 questions.

1

                A   B   C   D   E

2

                A   B   C   D   E

3

                A   B   C   D   E

4

                A   B   C   D   E

5

                A   B   C   D   E

6

                A   B   C   D   E

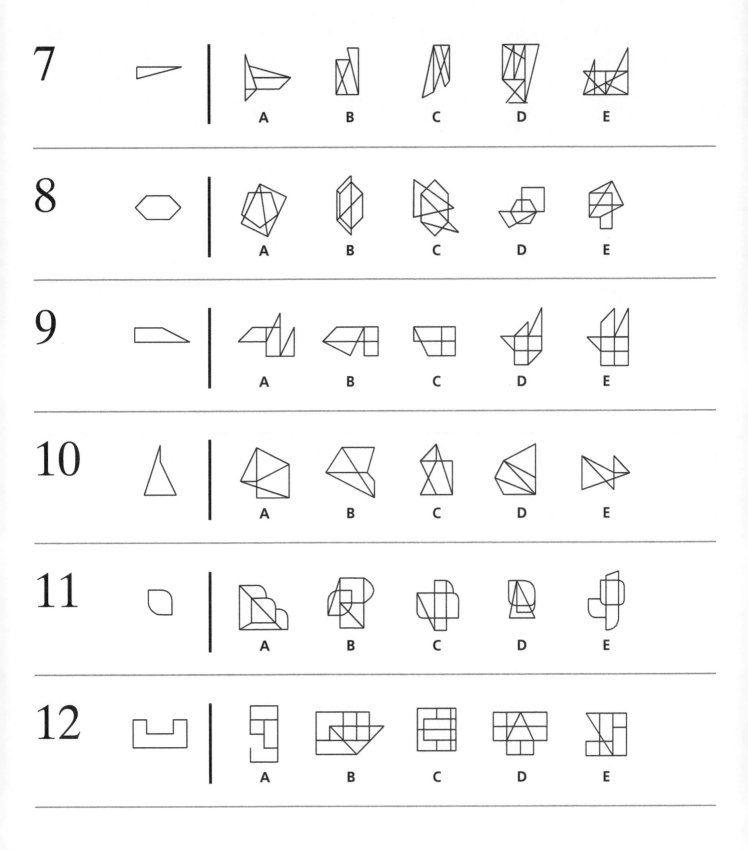

7   A   B   C   D   E

8   A   B   C   D   E

9   A   B   C   D   E

10   A   B   C   D   E

11   A   B   C   D   E

12   A   B   C   D   E

END OF PAPER

THIS PAGE HAS DELIBERATELY BEEN LEFT BLANK

Answers

Revision Answers

Making Connections
Page 17: Quick Test

1. a) E
        Triangle E is made up of dashed lines. The other triangles are made up of solid lines.
    b) E
        Shape E is a rectangle. The other shapes are all squares of differing sizes.
2. a) C
        Arrow C matches the two arrows on the left because it has an identical arrowhead. All the other arrows have different styles of arrowhead.
    b) E
        Triangle E matches the two triangles on the left because it is also an isosceles triangle.
3. a) C
        Shape C matches the two shapes on the left because it is also a white square made up of solid lines.
    b) A
        Image A matches the two images on the left because it also has two solid green segments and two spotted segments.
4. E
    Image E matches the two images on the left because it also has an alternating colour pattern (solid green squares follow white squares and white squares follow solid green squares). The arrow is a distraction.

Breaking Codes
Page 22: Quick Test

1. B
    A, C and B are the codes for the shading. M, L and N are the codes for the number of small squares. The fifth shape is spotted (C) and has three small squares (M). The answer is CM.
2. D
    D and E are the codes for the direction of the diagonal strip. H, I and J are the codes for the style of the top of the shield. X, Y and Z are the codes for the shading of the shield. The fifth shape has a diagonal strip that goes from top left to bottom right (E), the shield has three points at the top (I) and the shield is vertically striped (X). The answer is EIX.

Finding Relationships
Page 29: Quick Test

1. a) C
        The images in the boxes swap sizes and positions. There are no changes to the shading.
    b) B
        Squares become circles, circles become triangles and triangles become squares. Solid green shapes become white, white shapes become striped and striped shapes become solid green.

2. a) B
        The shapes in image B have a total of nine corners. This matches the number of corners in the two images on the left.
    b) E
        Image E also has three of its eight segments shaded in.
3. a) E
        The two small shapes move outside of the larger shape. The larger shape does not move.
    b) B
        The solid green shape slides up over the white shape until the patterns match up (join together).
4. a) B
        The shape in the box is reflected in a vertical mirror line.
    b) C
        In the first pair of images, the car body and roof change from white to solid green and the whole image is reflected in a vertical mirror line. In image C both the body and sail of the boat have been shaded solid green and reflected in a vertical mirror line.
5. a) E
        The image in the box is reflected in a horizontal mirror line.
    b) D
        The image in the box is reflected in a diagonal mirror line going from the bottom left to the top right.
    c) A
        The outer segments rotate 90° clockwise while the inner segments rotate 45° anti-clockwise.

Spotting Patterns
Page 34: Quick Test

1. B
    Moving across from left to right, the shape in each box gets smaller and the shading goes from solid green to white.
2. B
    The images in each box are reflected in a horizontal mirror line. The images at the bottom of the grid are a reflection of the images at the top.
3. E
    The top row contains three different sets of images. As you go down to the next row, the images move one box to the right. The images are also rotated 90° anti-clockwise.
4. C
    The first column of boxes is reflected in a vertical mirror line to make the last column of boxes and the shapes within them swap colours.

Completing Sequences
Page 41: Quick Test

1. B
    The triangle rotates 180° at each step and alternates between solid green and white.

2. D
    One of the circles is removed and a triangle is added in each box as the pattern moves from left to right. All the shapes alternate between solid green and white with each step.
3. E
    The solid circle moves one place around the star each time in a clockwise direction, stopping between the points.
4. C
    There are two patterns in this sequence. The first happens with every step – the image is reflected in a horizontal mirror line each time. The second happens with every other step – the solid green circle moves to the next point of the solid green triangle in an anti-clockwise direction in every other box.
5. D
    The number of triangles increases by three in each box from left to right.
6. B
    The number of circles decreases by two in each box from left to right.
7. C
    The number of items in each box matches the sequence of triangular numbers.

Spatial Reasoning
Page 47: Quick Test

1. a) D
        You can eliminate option A because the arrow would point to the black background with a white circle, not the small circle; option B because the arrow and the triangle are opposite one another when the net is folded; option C because the large and small circle are opposite one another when the net is folded; option E because the solid green triangle does not appear on the net.
    b) A
        You can eliminate option B because the small squares and the central line would be opposite one another when the net is folded; option C because the heart points away from the small squares rather than towards it; option D because the solid green circle does not appear on the net; option E because the square and the triangle are opposite one another when the net is folded.
2. a) B
        The rectangle appears in option B.
    b) D
        The irregular hexagon appears in option D.
3. a) E
        When the paper is unfolded, the holes would appear as shown.
    b) C
        When the paper is unfolded, the holes would appear as shown.
4. A rotates to form option iii.
    B rotates to form option i.
    C rotates to form option ii.

Pages 50–51
Practice Test 1: Making Connections

1. **E**

    All of the shapes have nine sides except for E, which has 11.

2. **A**

    All of the arrows point upwards except for A, which points downwards.

3. **D**

    All of the shapes have at least one line of symmetry except for D, which has no lines of symmetry.

4. **B**

    The circles all have one inner segment and one outer segment that is unshaded except for B.

5. **A**

    All of the shapes have straight line shading patterns except for shape A, which has a chequered pattern. It is also the only shape that contains right angles.

6. **C**

    The group of shapes in each of the first three boxes have 11 straight sides in total. Box C is the only one to match this.

7. **D**

    The first two shapes are isosceles triangles. Box D is the only one with an isosceles triangle in it.

8. **A**

    All of the individual shapes in the first two boxes have vertical lines of symmetry. Box A is the only other box where both shapes also have a vertical line of symmetry.

9. **B**

    The images are made up of a square surrounded by isosceles triangles. The triangles are split into two segments which are separated by their shading pattern. As you go clockwise around the image, the first segment of each triangle is shaded to match the square. The second segment of each triangle has a different shading pattern to the first segment. All of the second segments match each other.

10. **D**

    The car headlights on the first three images are all white. Car D is the only answer that matches this. All of the other shading and the position of the steering wheel are distractions.

11. **E**

    The first two boxes contain shapes with lines that are a regular dashed pattern. Shape E is the only shape with the same pattern.

Pages 52–53
Practice Test 2: Breaking Codes

1. **A**

    A, B and C are the codes for which point of the star is shaded – top, bottom left or bottom right. N, O and P are the codes for the shading – solid black, spotted or striped. The bottom-right point on the fifth star is shaded (C) and the shading pattern is spotted (O). The answer is CO.

2. **A**

    The first letter is for the type of star: D – four-pointed; F – five-pointed; E – six-pointed. The second letter is for

the shading pattern: S – vertical stripes; T – horizontal stripes; R – white. The orientation of the stars and patterns around their edges are distractions. The fifth shape is a five-pointed star (F) and white (R). The answer is FR.

3. **D**

    The images all look like the front of a car. The first letter is for the side the steering wheel is on: P – the steering wheel is on the left; Q – the steering wheel is on the right; R – the steering wheel is not visible. The second letter is for the body shading (but not the roof): T – white; S – black; U – spotted. The shading of the windscreen banner and the roof are distractions. The steering wheel on the fifth shape is on the right (Q) and has a white body (T). The answer is QT.

4. **C**

    The first letter is for the shape of the top of the shield: G – double curve; E – straight; F – single curve. The second letter describes the number of shapes on the shield: K – two shapes; J – three shapes; L – four shapes. The shading on the shields is a distraction. The fifth shape has a single curve on the shield (F) and has three shapes inside it (J). The answer is FJ.

5. **C**

    The first letter is for the tail of the arrow: E – one fin; D – no fins; F – two fins. The second letter describes the head of the arrow: P – diamond head; Q – round head; O – triangular head. The orientation of the arrows is a distraction. The fifth shape has two fins (F) and a diamond head (P). The answer is FP.

6. **E**

    The first letter is for the combination of shapes: V – circle and pentagon; U – square and triangle; W – circle and triangle. The second letter is for the shading: A – vertical stripes; C – horizontal stripes; B – spotted. The position of the shapes is a distraction. The fifth image has a square and triangle (U) and is spotted (B). The answer is UB.

7. **C**

    The first letter is for the shading of the centre of the image: C – black; A – spotted; B – white. The second letter is for the orientation: E – vertical/horizontal; F – diagonal. The third letter is for the shading of the triangles: I – white; J – spotted; H – black. The fifth shape has a spotted centre (A), has a diagonal orientation (F) and the triangles are shaded black (H). The answer is AFH.

8. **B**

    The first letter is for the shading of the second half of each triangle as you go in a clockwise direction around the image: O – black; Q – striped; P – white. The second letter is for the shading at the centre of the image: R – striped; T – black; S – white. The third letter is for the shading of the first half of each triangle as you go in a clockwise direction around the image: W – white; U – spotted; V – black. The fifth image has the second half of each triangle shaded black (O), the centre

of the image is black (T) and the first half of the triangle is black (V). The answer is OTV.

9. **A**

    The first letter is the shading on the top triangle of the star: V – striped; W – spotted; U – black. The second letter is for a vertical line of symmetry: O – there is a vertical line of symmetry; P – there is no vertical line of symmetry. The third letter is for the shading on the lowest two triangles: D – chequered; B – striped; C – white. The shading of the pentagon in the middle and the higher two triangles are distractions. The fifth shape has a black triangle at the top (U), a vertical line of symmetry (O) and the lower triangles are chequered (D). The answer is UOD.

10. **B**

    The first letter is for the middle block of each image: E – no shading; F – striped; G – spotted. The second letter is for the bottom block: L – black; M – striped; K – spotted. The third letter is for the top block: S – striped; U – black; T – spotted. The fifth shape has a striped middle block (F), a spotted bottom block (K) and a spotted top block (T). The answer is FKT.

11. **E**

    The first letter describes whether the arrow is pointing up or down: B – down; A – up. The second letter is for the style of the arrowhead: C – triangular head; D – diamond head; E – round head. The third letter describes whether the arrow is pointing left or right: G – left; F – right. The fifth shape is pointing down (B), has a round arrowhead (E) and is pointing to the left (G). The answer is BEG.

12. **E**

    The first letter is for the basic shape: N – triangle; M – quadrilateral; O – pentagon. The second letter is for whether or not the shape is regular: C – irregular; B – regular. The third letter is for the shading of the shape: Y – spotted; Z – black; X – striped. The fifth shape is a pentagon (O), is irregular (C) and is shaded black (Z). The answer is OCZ.

13. **B**

    The images all look like houses. The first letter is for whether or not the house has a chimney: F – it has a chimney; G – it does not have a chimney. The second letter is for the number of floors: L – one floor; M – two floors; K – three floors. The third letter is for the shading of the roof: U – white; V – striped; T – black. The fifth shape has a chimney (F), two floors (M) and a black roof (T). The answer is FMT.

14. **E**

    The images all look like a boat at sea. The first letter is for the wave style: B – the waves are pointed; D – there are no waves; C – the waves are curved. The second letter is for the sail: I – the sail is pointing to the right; H – the sail is pointing to the left. The third letter is for the colour of the hull of the boat: V – black; W – striped; X – spotted. The fifth shape has no waves (D), a sail pointing to the left (H) and a spotted hull (X). The answer is DHX.

Pages 54–55
Practice Test 3: Finding Relationships

1. **A**
The shape in the top left-hand corner changes to match the size and shape of the bottom-right corner shape, although it retains its original shading pattern. The larger of the two other shapes moves under the smaller one and they swap shading patterns.

2. **C**
The square changes into a star with the same number of points. The points of the star are along a line from the centre of the original square through the middle of each side. As the pentagon has a horizontal edge at the top, the star must point straight up.

3. **B**
The image rotates 90° clockwise. The shading pattern on the middle segment swaps with the other segments. The angle of the pattern is rotated with the image. The thickness of the lines does not change.

4. **D**
The segments rotate and join together to form a larger shape. The segments stay in the same area of the box.

5. **B**
The segments fold out and the shading moves one segment clockwise.

6. **E**
The shapes are reflected in a vertical mirror line and, after the reflection, the shading styles move to the next shape anti-clockwise.

7. **D**
The image is reflected in a vertical mirror line and the shading style of the shapes within it swaps with that of the background.

8. **B**
The shapes are reflected in a horizontal mirror line running through the middle of the box. The shading in the group of four shapes moves one shape to the right, while the shading in the group of three shapes moves one shape to the left. The shading patterns are not reflected.

9. **E**
The image is reflected in a horizontal mirror line.

10. **C**
The whole box is reflected in a horizontal mirror line. Once reflected, the shading pattern moves to the next shape in an anti-clockwise direction.

11. **C**
The box is reflected in a diagonal mirror line going from bottom left to top right. The segmented shape is a distraction as it doesn't look like it has been reflected at all, merely translated.

12. **A**
The box is reflected in a diagonal mirror line going from top left to bottom right.

13. **D**
The shading patterns on the outer segments of the image rotate 90° clockwise while the shading patterns on the inner segments rotate 90° anti-clockwise.

14. **C**
The shape rotates 90° anti-clockwise and the shading changes from black to white.

Pages 56–57
Practice Test 4: Spotting Patterns

1. **D**
The line in the second column becomes a corner before it moves to the first column. The other shape is turned into a regular shape, keeping the same height as the original. There is still a gap between the shape and the corner/line.

2. **B**
To get from the top row to the bottom row, the shapes are reflected in a horizontal mirror line and the shading changes. If it was white it becomes black, and if it was black it becomes white.

3. **C**
The images in the first column are reflected in a vertical mirror line into the second column.

4. **A**
All the segments of the star that were white in the first column are spotted in the second column. The segments that were spotted become black and the ones that were black become white.

5. **C**
The image in the first column is taken apart in the second column. For the 'clock' image this means that the circle for the face, the hand section, the pendulum arm and the pendulum itself are all separated. Nothing is rotated.

6. **E**
The grid has a vertical mirror line running down the middle of the second column. The first column is reflected in that line to become the third column before being shaded black.

7. **C**
From one row to the next, the shapes move one box to the right but the shading patterns move one box to the left. All of the first row shapes are in the top left of their boxes, the second row shapes are in the middle of their boxes and the bottom row shapes are in the bottom right of their boxes.

8. **A**
The shapes in each box work as one image. Each image moves down to the next row, moves one box to the left and rotates 90° clockwise.

Pages 58–59
Practice Test 5: Completing Sequences

1. **C**
The shapes in the box alternate between a striped circle and a grey oval. The missing shape is a grey oval.

2. **D**
The shapes are symmetrical in a vertical mirror line that goes through the third box, so the shapes in the second and fourth boxes are identical and the shapes in the first and last box should be identical. The missing shape is a spotted square.

3. **D**
The shapes all look like regular shapes that have been squashed horizontally. Going from left to right, the shapes lose one side in each box. The missing shape is a tall pentagon. The shading is a distraction.

4. **B**
The shading pattern inside the diamond rotates 45° anti-clockwise in each box. The missing shape is a diamond with vertically striped shading. The arrows are a distraction.

5. **A**
Moving left to right, two squares are removed from each box and an octagon is added at the top. The squares are removed from the top, working from left to right on each row.

6. **C**
The triangle is reflected in a horizontal mirror line in each box. Whenever it points upwards it is white in colour; when it points down it is shaded black. The pentagon is reflected in a horizontal mirror line in every second box, with the direction of the striped shading reflecting as well.

7. **E**
The shading pattern of the inner segments rotates one segment clockwise while the shading of the outer segments rotates one segment anti-clockwise. The outer shape switches between being a circle and a square.

8. **D**
The boxes alternate between a growing square pattern and a repeating circle pattern. The circles rotate around the box in an anti-clockwise direction, while the squares go in a clockwise direction.

9. **C**
Moving left to right, the squares move from the bottom to the top of each box and back again. The black square moves one along to the right. The circles do not move but the spotted shading moves one circle clockwise while the black one moves two circles anti-clockwise. When the same circle should have both types of shading only the black is seen.

10. **A**
Moving left to right, one circle becomes a triangle. The triangle closest to the edge of the box changes its shading between white and black each time and the other triangles alternate along the line. The whole shape rotates 90° anti-clockwise from one box to the next.

11. **B**
Moving left to right, the number of shapes in each box decreases by three each time. The shapes alternate between four- and five-pointed stars.

12. **D**
The number of shapes in each box is two more than the last. The specific shapes are distractions.

13. **B**
The boxes have the sequence of square numbers in them with 25 shapes in the first box, 16 in the second and so on. There should be nine shapes in the empty box. The shading of all the shapes inside any box should be the same. The specific shapes are distractions.

14. **E**
The boxes alternate between having triangles and squares in them. The number of shapes is the sequence of

triangular numbers so the fourth box should have ten squares in it. Neither squares nor triangles rotate, which excludes option B. The shading patterns are a distraction.

Pages 60–61
Practice Test 6: Spatial Reasoning
1. **D**
When the net is folded, the oval will touch the two triangles as shown. You can eliminate option A as there is no small black square on the net; option B because the black squares on the front face appear in the opposite positions to what they would be; option C because the oval and the black circle have swapped places compared to where they would be when the net was folded; option E because the two large black triangles would be opposite one another when the net was folded.
2. **C**
When the net is folded, the two lines with dots would be positioned as shown and the double line would run vertically on the right-hand face. You can eliminate option A because it shows a horizontal, not diagonal, line with white circles; option B because it shows an unhappy face, not a smiling one; option D because it shows two lines with black dots; option E because it shows a black diamond, not a white one.
3. **A**
When the net is folded, the three faces will touch as shown. You can eliminate option B because the black and the white flat-ended lollipops have their bases touching rather than being parallel with one another; option C because the black and the white circles are in the wrong position; option D because the multiplication signs and one of the black and white circle patterns are opposite each other when the net is folded; option E because the plus signs and the white flat-ended lollipop appear on the wrong faces if the net is folded as shown.
4. **D**
When the net is folded, the faces can touch one another as shown. You can eliminate option A because it has two fine plus signs; option B because the two chunky plus signs would appear swapped round if the cube were folded as shown; option C because the two chunky multiplication signs are opposite one another when the net is folded; option E because the bold black plus sign and the fine plus sign are opposite one another when the net is folded.
5. **E**
When the net is folded, the faces can touch as shown. You can eliminate options A and B because the right-hand face would be diagonal stripes, not solid black; option C because the triangles do not appear on the net; option D because the diagonal striped squares will be folded into the cube so that the shaded quarters do not touch directly, but instead they touch the white quarters.
6. **C**
The right-angled triangle appears in option C.

7. **A**
The irregular hexagon appears in option A.
8. **C**
The isosceles triangle appears in option C.
9. **B**
The irregular quadrilateral appears in option B.
10. **B**
The circle appears in option B.

Pages 62–69
Practice Test 7: Mixed Practice
1. **B**
The images are made up of three similar shapes, the medium shape having a striped shading pattern. The stripes in shape B go in the opposite direction.
2. **C**
All the shapes have six sides except for C, which has five sides.
3. **A**
All of the angles are acute other than A, which is obtuse.
4. **E**
The only shape with a straight side in it is shape E.
5. **D**
The only circle without a line through the middle is circle D. The style of the line is a distraction.
6. **D**
All of the shapes have an even number of sides except for D, which is a triangle and has three sides (an odd number).
7. **C**
Q, P and R are the codes for the shape – a curve that looks like it takes a bite out of the rectangle, a rectangle, a curve that turns the rectangle into a 'D' shape. S, T and U are the codes for the shading – spotted, black or white. The fifth shape is a curve that goes into the rectangle (Q) and is white (U). The answer is QU.
8. **B**
K, L and M are the codes for the shading of the outer segments – black and white, black and striped, white and striped. Z, X, and Y are the codes for the shading of the inner segments – black and spotted, spotted and striped, black and white. The fifth image is shaded black and striped in the outer segments (L), black and spotted in the inner segments (Z). The answer is LZ.
9. **C**
K, L and J are the codes for the number of small triangles – three, four or two. T, U and V are the codes for the direction the small triangles are pointing – up, down or right. The fifth shape has four small triangles (L) pointing to the right (V). The answer is LV.
10. **E**
D, E and F are the codes for the shading of the inner segments – black and white, black and striped or white and striped. H, J and I are the codes for the shading of the outer segments – black and white, white and striped or black and striped. N, O and M are the codes for the crosses – whether they do not overlap, overlap and are diagonal or overlap and are vertical. The fifth shape has black and striped inner segments (E), black and striped

outer segments (I), and the crosses do not overlap (N). The answer is EIN.
11. **A**
A, B and C are the codes for which point is shaded black – top, bottom left or bottom right. I, J and H are the codes for which other segment is shaded – I is top right, J is bottom right, H is top left. O, P and N are the codes for the shading of the non-black point – spotted, striped or chequered. The fifth shape's black point is in the bottom left (B), the other shaded segment is in the bottom right (J) and it has spotted shading (O). The correct answer is BJO.
12. **B**
Sections of the image that had a diagonal pattern that went down and to the right are given a pattern with horizontal lines. Sections of the image that had a diagonal pattern that went up and to the right are given a pattern with vertical lines.
13. **C**
The shapes within the box stay in the same position but the shading changes. The shapes that were black become striped, those that were striped become white, and those that were white become black.
14. **C**
The first box has four three-sided shapes; this changes into three four-sided shapes (i.e. the total number of sides stays the same). The five four-sided shapes become four five-sided shapes.
15. **E**
The segments of the image that were white become spotted, those that were spotted become black, and those that were black become white.
16. **E**
The three identical lines within the box build an equilateral triangle so the four identical lines build a square.
17. **A**
The shapes in the first box are joined together and the shape in the middle is shaded black. The outside shapes are not rotated.
18. **D**
The whole box is reflected in a vertical mirror line.
19. **E**
The box is reflected in a diagonal mirror line going from top left to bottom right.
20. **A**
The black rectangle stays in the same half of the square and the black triangles take the places of the white and striped triangles (which also swap shading between the top half of the square and the bottom).
21. **D**
The image is rotated 135° clockwise; the line goes from being solid to being dashed.
22. **C**
As the image in the box moves from left to right, the two small shapes swap places and then the whole image, including the small shapes, is reflected in a vertical mirror line.
23. **D**
The triangles in the left-hand box are brought together in the right-hand box and the space in between them is shaded black.

24. E

The shapes in the left-hand box have the same number of corners (or sides) as the shapes in the right-hand box. The top row have 20, the bottom row have 12.

25. C

As the images move down a row, they rotate 45° clockwise and move one box to the left.

26. A

The first column has small white shapes in the top left corner of the boxes. The last column has large black shapes in the bottom right corner of the boxes. The middle column contains an image in the centre of the box made up of the white shape in the middle of the black shape. The images rotate 90° clockwise from one column to the next.

27. C

The circle gets smaller from left to right. The colour alternates from box to box.

28. B

The pentagons get bigger from left to right. The shading pattern changes from black to white to spotted, then black (in the missing box) and back to white. The pentagons also rotate 90° anti-clockwise in each box.

29. A

The pattern is symmetrical about the middle box. The image in the second box will be identical to the one in the fourth box.

30. B

The boxes all show a series of discs, some from the side and some from face on. The smallest disc is removed as you go across the boxes.

31. A

The shading in the outer segments of each image rotates one segment anti-clockwise, while the shading in the inner segments rotates one segment clockwise.

32. E

As you move one box to the right, the black circle is replaced with a triangle. The next circle in a clockwise direction is turned black. A white circle is added in the bottom left and a triangle is removed from the top right.

33. C

The images alternate between squares and circles, but all are in eight segments. The shading of the outer segments rotates one segment clockwise, and the angle of the striped shading rotates anti-clockwise about the middle of the shapes as it moves. The shaded inner segment rotates one segment anti-clockwise each time.

34. D

The number of sides in each shape increases by one in each box from left to right. The shapes also alternate between solid and dashed lines.

35. D

The number of shapes in each box is the (decreasing) sequence of square numbers from 25 to 1. The shapes in each box gain one side from one box to the next.

36. D

When viewed from above, the figure shows two cubes in the front row, with one cube in the middle row and one cube in the back row. The middle and back cubes are aligned to the right-hand side of the front row.

37. D

When viewed from above, the figure shows three cubes in the front row, with one cube in the back row (aligned with the right-hand side of the front row).

38. A

When viewed from above, the figure shows four cubes in the front row, with two cubes in the back row, aligned with the far left-hand side and second cube from the right-hand side of the front row.

39. E

When viewed from above, the figure shows four cubes in the front row and five cubes in the back row, aligned so that the additional cube on the back row is on the right-hand side.

40. D

When viewed from above, the figure shows four cubes in the front row and two cubes in the back row, centrally positioned. The answer cannot be B because you can see from the right-hand side of the figure that there is no cube on the far right-hand side of the back row.

41. E

When the paper is unfolded, the holes would appear as shown.

42. D

When the paper is unfolded, the holes would appear as shown.

43. D

When the paper is unfolded, the holes would appear as shown.

44. C

When the paper is unfolded, the holes would appear as shown.

45. E

When the paper is unfolded, the holes would appear as shown.

46. D

When the paper is unfolded, the holes would appear as shown.

Assessment Answers

PRACTICE PAPER 1
Pages 74–76: Paper 1, Section 1

1. E

In the first pair, the left-hand image rotates 90° anti-clockwise to produce the right-hand image. Making the same change for the second pair means that E is the correct answer.

2. A

In the first pair, the shapes swap positions and the lower shape retains the striped pattern. The lower shape in the left-hand image is also reflected in a horizontal line. Making the same changes for the second pair means that A is the correct answer.

3. B

In the first pair, the shading moves down one row and the whole shape becomes wider. Making the same changes for the second pair means that B is the correct answer.

4. B

In the first pair, the two large semi-circles in the left-hand image become the small, inner shapes in the right-hand image. The two small triangles in the left-hand image become the large, outer shapes in the right-hand image. The shading is also reversed. Making the same changes for the second pair means that B is the correct answer.

5. C

In the first pair, the left-hand image is rotated 180° to produce the second image. Making the same change for the second pair means that C is the correct answer.

6. B

In the first pair, the left-hand image is reflected in a vertical line to produce the second image. Making the same change for the second pair means that B is the correct answer.

7. E

In the first pair, the inner shape in the left-hand image becomes the outer shape in the right-hand image, while the outer shape becomes the inner one. Both shapes retain their shading patterns. Making the same changes for the second pair means that E is the correct answer.

8. D

In the first pair, the image is rotated 180° and, at the same time, the lower shape moves into a position where it is in contact with the other shape. Making the same changes for the second pair means that D is the correct answer.

9. A

In the first pair, the left-hand image is rotated 90° anti-clockwise and is then reflected in a horizontal line to produce the right-hand image. Making the same changes for the second pair means that A is the correct answer.

10. E

In the first pair, the three shapes are combined with the two smaller shapes fitting inside the largest shape. The smallest shape is placed inside the middle-sized shape. Making the same changes for the second pair means that E is the correct answer.

11. D

In the first pair, the pentagon is reflected in a vertical line and reduced in size. The quadrilateral inside the pentagon swaps positions with the black circle and is reduced, while the circle remains at the same size. Making the same changes for the second pair means that D is the correct answer.

12. E

In the first pair, the left-image has a central black circle surrounded by six white circles. To produce the right-hand image, the black circle enlarges and encloses a six-sided shape, i.e. a hexagon. In the second pair, you can expect the central black square to enlarge and enclose a four-sided shape (since there are four white circles around it). Therefore E is the correct answer.

1. **E**
   The squares decrease in size from left to right and the shading alternates, therefore E is the correct answer.

2. **D**
   The image rotates 90° clockwise at each step from left to right. D (rather than A) is correct because the striped pattern in the triangle runs parallel to the black rectangle as it does in the sequence.

3. **A**
   At each step of the sequence, from left to right, the shapes move one place around the square in an anti-clockwise direction. Therefore A is correct.

4. **C**
   This is an alternating sequence of concentric circles and a cross. From right to left, the black shading in the concentric circles is moving outwards at each step, so C is the correct answer.

5. **A**
   From right to left, the semi-circle moves anti-clockwise around the sides of the square alternating between black and white shading as it does so. From right to left, the pair of circles move clockwise around the sides of the square, while the shading of the 'single' circle changes from black to white to a cross (so a single white circle will appear in the answer).

6. **E**
   From left to right, the line extends by half a length and the black circle moves with it on the inside. Therefore E is correct.

7. **D**
   From left to right, the black shading in the octagon moves two segments in a clockwise direction at each step. The white circle does likewise but the black circle only moves one segment clockwise at each step. The black square moves around the corners of the square in an anti-clockwise direction at each step. Therefore D is correct.

8. **D**
   From left to right, the number of dots and the number of lines in each square increase in sequence with the triangular numbers (1, 3, 6, 10, 15, …). Therefore the answer has 6 dots in a triangular formation and a total of 10 lines at the corners.

9. **B**
   From left to right, the triangle rotates 90° as it moves clockwise around the grid and its shading alternates between black and white. The white circle alternates in position between the bottom left and top right of the grid at each step. Therefore B is correct.

10. **E**
    From left to right, the black circle moves clockwise around the corners of the square while the number of sides of the polygon increases by one at each step. The polygons also increase in size. Therefore the answer is a hexagon with the black circle positioned in the bottom right corner.

11. **E**
    Starting from the left, there are two sets of concentric triangles – one set with two triangles and one set with three triangles. At each step, the two sets move anti-clockwise around the corners of the square and rotate 90°. After every two steps, the inner triangle of each concentric pair disappears, meaning that in the final box one of the concentric sets will disappear altogether and the remaining large white triangle will rotate to fill the upper left part of the square.

12. **B**
    From left to right, the arrow and the triangle shapes rotate 45° as they move clockwise around the square. The other two shapes continue to face each other at each step. B is the only option where the arrow and the triangle are both in the correct positions.

1. **B**
   In the first row, the left-hand image reflects in a vertical line to create the image on the right. At the same time, the shading of the central shape changes from white to black. Applying the same changes to the second row means that B is correct.

2. **C**
   As you move down each row, the shapes move one column to the left and the black shading on each moves towards the inside until it reaches the centre, at which point it reverts to the outside. Therefore the answer is a set of concentric circles with the circle second from the outside shaded black.

3. **C**
   In the first row, the large shape in the left-hand image rotates 90° clockwise to create the right-hand image. The smaller shape moves from the top left-hand corner to a position within the larger shape and the shading of both shapes is reversed. Applying the same changes to the second row means that C is correct.

4. **D**
   As you move from the top row downwards, the shapes move one column to the left and become larger. The shapes in the middle row are also rotated 90° compared with the top and bottom rows. Therefore the answer is a hexagon that is rotated 90° from its position in the top and bottom rows.

5. **B**
   As you move from the top row downwards, one black shape disappears at each step. Therefore the answer is the option with one white triangle and one black triangle.

6. **A**
   In the first row, the left-hand image reflects in a vertical line to create the image on the right. Applying the same change to the second row means that A is correct.

7. **E**
   In each row, the image in the middle column is created by the shape in the first column combining with the shape in the third column. The shape in the third column undergoes a 90° anti-clockwise rotation when it appears in the middle column and overlaps the shape from the first column, meaning that E is correct.

8. **B**
   In the second row, the left-hand image is reflected in a vertical line to produce the right-hand image. At the same time, the shading reverses in the upper and lower shapes. Applying the same changes to the first row means that B is correct.

9. **B**
   Moving left to right from the first column, the shapes rotate 45° clockwise. Applying this change to the middle row means that B is correct.

10. **E**
    Moving left to right from the first column, the shapes rotate 90° clockwise, enlarge and move from the bottom left of the square towards the top right. Applying this change to the middle row means that E is correct.

11. **D**
    Moving from the top row downwards, the shapes move one column to the right and one extra segment is shaded black. The shading of the segments and the position of the black circle is the same in each row. Therefore the correct answer has the bottom left and top right segments shaded black, and the black circle positioned in the bottom right segment.

12. **A**
    The upper image of the first column is reflected in a horizontal line to produce the lower image. Applying the same change in the second column means that A is correct.

1. **D**
   The two images on the left only have curved lines, therefore D is correct.

2. **E**
   The two images on the left show a circle surrounded on half of its side by one outer shape, therefore E is correct.

3. **D**
   The two images on the left are both rotated 'H' shapes, therefore D is correct.

4. **A**
   The two images on the left both show a circle with three smaller shapes – one is a square and the other two shapes are identical (one of these overlaps the edge of the circle). Therefore A, which shows the circle with one square and two triangles, is correct.

5. **E**
   In the two images on the left, the longer sides of the wider 'L' shape are on the sides left 'open' by the thinner 'L' shape. Therefore E is correct.

6. **C**
   In each of the two images on the left, three identical shapes are linked together like a chain. Therefore C is the correct answer with three triangles linked in the same way.

7. **D**
   Both of the images on the left have four white circles within a polygon. The black circles are a distraction. Therefore D, the only option with four white circles, is the correct answer.

8. **B**
   The images on the left show one square

inside a larger square and one circle inside a larger circle. The style of the outlines is a distraction. The correct answer is B because it is the only option with one shape inside a larger version of the same shape (in this case a hexagon).

9. **D**
Both shapes on the left are octagons. The correct answer is D because this is the only octagon among the options.

10. **E**
The images on the left show a set of triangles and a set of squares. In each set, there is a concentric pair of shapes and two single shapes, with the larger of the two single shapes placed at the top right. B and E are the only options where the shapes are the same kind within the set, but E is correct because the larger single shape is correctly placed at the top right.

11. **A**
The two images on the left show two identical shapes overlapping at the same point on both shapes. A is correct because this is the only option that shows two identical shapes overlapping at the same point on both shapes (B and E do not overlap at the same point on each shape).

12. **C**
The two images on the left both have an odd number of black circles and an odd number of 'ear-like' extensions. C is correct because this is the only option with an odd number of black circles (1) and an odd number of extensions (3).

Pages 86–88: Paper 1, Section 5

1. **B**
The upper letter is the code for the position of the arc and this is 'S' for the given image. The lower letter is the code for the shading of the circle, so 'K' is a white circle.

2. **D**
The upper letter is the code for the number of white shapes in the square and this is 'R' for the given image. The lower letter is the code for the size of the black circle, so 'K' is the code for a small circle.

3. **C**
The upper letter is the code for the number of crosses inside the central shape and this is 'J' for the given image. The lower letter is the code for the central shape, so 'M' is for an oval.

4. **D**
The upper letter is the code for the shading pattern of the pair of arches, so this is 'T' for the given image. The lower letter is the code for the style of the dividing line, so 'Y' is the code for a line split into two halves.

5. **A**
The upper letter is the code for the position of the parallel lines and this is 'Z' for the given image. The lower letter is the code for the number of black triangles, so 'N' is for one triangle.

6. **D**
The upper letter is the code for the shading of the shape and this is 'N' for the given image. The lower letter is the code for the shape, so 'X' is for a triangle.

7. **E**
The upper letter is the code for the pattern of the roof and this is 'H' for the given image. The lower letter is the code for the shape of the building, so that is 'Z' for the given image.

8. **D**
The upper letter is the code for the position of the white triangle and this is 'N' for the given image. The lower letter is the code for the position of the black triangle, so 'Y' is when it is in the upper position.

9. **A**
The upper letter is the code for the orientation of the black line and this is 'T' for the given image. The lower letter is the code for the number of white circles, so that is 'Y' for one circle.

10. **B**
The upper letter is the code for the shape and this is 'P' for the given image. The lower letter is the code for the number of sections that the shape is divided into, so 'N' is for two sections.

11. **D**
The upper letter is the code for the size of the triangle and this is 'X' for the given image. The lower letter is the code for the length of the lined pattern, so 'M' is the code for the shortest.

12. **D**
The upper letter is the code for the orientation and shape of the larger figure and this is 'J' for the diamond in the given image. The lower letter is the code for the number of white triangles at each corner, so 'M' is the code for only one of these. The black shapes are a distraction.

PRACTICE PAPER 2
Pages 90–92: Paper 2, Section 1

1. **A**
The answer is A because it does not fit into the same rotation pattern as the others.

2. **E**
The answer is E because the position of the white circle and the white triangle is different to the others.

3. **D**
The answer is D because it is the only option where the black rectangle overlaps in front of the white rectangle.

4. **E**
The answer is E because the black shape has curved sides to match the curved style of the patterned side of the white shape. The other options have a combination of curvy-sided black shapes with white shapes that have a straight-lined style on the patterned side, or vice-versa.

5. **E**
The answer is E because it is the only option with an even number of white, circular features and an odd number of black, circular features. The other options all have an odd number of white features and an even number of black features.

6. **D**
The answer is D because it is the only option where the shape that forms the 'mouth' is not fully aligned vertically with the pair of 'eyes'.

7. **A**
The answer is A because in all the other options the shading of the outer shapes alternates from black to white; in option A there are two white circles positioned next to each other.

8. **C**
The answer is C because in the other options the circle overlaps a corner on a shape with an odd number of sides and overlaps a side only on shapes with an even number of sides.

9. **A**
The answer is A because it is the only option where the two shapes could be rotated to fit exactly one over the other.

10. **B**
The answer is B because the white circle is placed to the other side of the black segment compared with the other options.

11. **E**
The answer is E because it is the only option where the square is divided into four smaller squares (rather than into four small triangles).

12. **D**
The answer is D because it is the only option where the image does not have a vertical line of reflection.

Pages 93–95: Paper 2, Section 2

1. **D**
When the net is folded, the black triangle on the front face will touch the cross which forms the upper face of the cube. The black rectangle will be at the back of the right-hand face. You can eliminate option A as the black rectangle does not touch the cross with a long side; option B because the cross and the triangle are on the wrong faces; option C as the small cross does not appear on the net; and option E as the two crosses are opposite one another when the net is folded.

2. **A**
When the net is folded with the concentric circles on the top face, the small white circle will be on the front and the small black circle on the right-hand face as shown. You can eliminate option B as the large and concentric circles are opposite one another when the net is folded; option C as the large black circle is not shown on the net; option D as the small black circle and the smiley face will be opposite one another; and option E because the large white circle and the concentric circles are opposite one another.

3. **A**
When the net is folded with the stripes on the front face as shown, the black diamond is on the top face and the small white circle on the right-hand face. You can eliminate option B because the black square does not appear on the net; option C because the rectangle and the small circle are opposite when the net is folded; option D because the stripes and the small black circle with the diagonal line are opposite when the net is folded; and option E because the single black circle does not appear on the net.

4. E

When the net is folded with the small black triangles as shown on the cube in E, the black lemon shapes will be on the top face. You can eliminate option A because the black lemon shapes and the bold stripe would be opposite one another when the net is folded; option B because the white lemon shapes and the black triangle will be opposite one another; option C because the white lemons and the dashed line would be perpendicular to one another rather than parallel; and option D because the bold line would be pointing towards the black triangle.

5. B

When the net is folded with the two triangles as shown on the front face, the circles would be on the top face and the black rectangle on the right-hand side. You can eliminate option A as the black rectangle and the black square will be opposite each other when the net is folded; option C as the black rectangle will touch the stripes along one of its shorter sides; option D as the square and the rectangle will be opposite one another when the net is folded; option E as the stripes and the circles will be opposite one another when the net is folded.

6. B

When the net is folded with the triangle on the front face as shown, the black scallops will be on the top face and the white scallops on the right-hand face. You can eliminate option A because the two black and white squared faces have alternating black and white sections, not touching; option C because the black scallops point away from the black triangle; option D because the white triangle points towards the black scallops; option E because the black and white squares are in the opposite places to how they are shown on the net.

7. E

When the net is folded with the long single line horizontal on the front face, the short single line will be on the top face and the white arrow will point down on the right-hand face. You can eliminate option A as the black-headed arrow and the fine arrow do not point at one another; option B because there are not two white arrows; option C because the white arrow would point down rather than up; and option D because the short single line and the black-headed arrow are opposite one another.

8. C

When the net is folded with the four-pointed black star on the front face, the black heart will be on the top face and the white heart on the right-hand face as shown. You can eliminate options A and D because the black heart and the black five-pointed star are opposite when the net is folded; option B because the four-pointed stars are opposite one another when the net is folded; and option E because the hearts point at one another.

9. E

When the net is folded, the parallel lines will touch the short black lines and the rectangle as shown in E. You can eliminate option A as the parallel lines are shown in the opposite direction to how they would be if the cube was folded; option B because the four-pointed star does not appear on the net; option C because the rectangle would be on the left-hand face, not the right-hand face; and option D because the oval and the star have been swapped compared to how they would actually be when the net is folded.

10. A

When the net is folded as shown in A, the irregular pentagon would be on the front face pointing towards the regular hexagon on the right-hand face and the black shield would be on the top face, pointing left. You can eliminate option B because the arrowhead would be on the bottom face (hidden) if the cube was positioned as shown; option C because there is not a regular white pentagon on the net; option D because the white shield would be on the left-hand face (hidden) if the cube was positioned as shown; and option E because the white shield does not point to the curved part of the black shield.

11. A

When the net is folded as shown in A, the bold arrowhead will point to the square, with the bold cross to the right-hand side. You can eliminate option B because the bold line and the fine arrowhead have swapped places compared to how they would be if the net was folded; options C and D because the bold arrowhead points away from the bold line; and option E because the dashed line would originate from the corner between the square and the fine arrowhead, not the opposite corner as shown.

12. D

When the net is folded as shown in D, the black equilateral triangle points to the large white equilateral triangle. You can eliminate option A because the black triangle points to the black circle, not the large white equilateral triangle; option B because the concentric triangle should be parallel with the side that joins the black circle; option C because the black triangle is not pointing to the large white equilateral triangle; and option E because the black isosceles triangle would be on the left-hand face (hidden).

Pages 96–98: Paper 2, Section 3

1. C

In the first pair, the left-hand image is reflected in a vertical line to produce the right-hand image. Making the same change for the second pair means that C is the correct answer.

2. A

In the first pair, the pair of semi-circles in the left-hand image become triangles in the right-hand image but the inner black triangle reverses its orientation compared with the larger triangle. Making the same changes for the second pair (this time using two pairs of semi-circles but with the inner ones reversed in orientation compared with the outer ones) means that A is the correct answer.

3. A

In the first pair, the left-hand image rotates 90° clockwise and the shading pattern swaps between the two parts of the image. Making the same changes for the second pair means that A is the correct answer.

4. E

In the first pair, the three pieces of the left-hand image rotate and come apart. Making the same change for the second pair means that E (with the correct-shaped and shaded pieces) is the correct answer.

5. D

In the first pair, the two shapes in the left-hand image swap places to create the right-hand image. At the same time, the white triangle reflects in a horizontal line and its original position is filled with the black shading of the square block. Making the same changes for the second pair means that D is the correct answer.

6. C

In the first pair, the 'L' shape of the left-hand image rotates 90° anti-clockwise and the 'n' shape rotates 90° clockwise to create the right-hand image. Making the same changes for the second pair means that C is the correct answer.

7. B

In the first pair, the shapes in the left-hand image are rotated 90° and duplicated for the right-hand image so that one pair is positioned top left and one pair is positioned bottom right. At the same time, the shapes reduce in size and swap shading patterns. Making the same changes for the second pair means that B is the correct answer.

8. C

In the first pair, the left-hand image reflects in a horizontal line to produce the right-hand image. At the same time, the square and the circle swap places and the shading stays in the bottom half of the image. Making the same changes for the second pair means that C is the correct answer.

9. D

In the first pair, the pieces of the left-hand image come apart and rotate approximately 45° anti-clockwise to produce the right-hand image. Making the same changes for the second pair means that D is the correct answer.

10. E

In the first pair, the left-hand image rotates 135° clockwise to produce the right-hand image. Making the same change for the second pair means that E is the correct answer.

11. A

In the first pair, the left-hand image rotates 150° anti-clockwise to produce the right-hand image. Making the same change for the second pair means that A is the correct answer.

12. E

In the first pair, the triangle in the left-hand image enlarges and moves so that it overlaps the right-hand side of the circle. The triangle is then reflected in a vertical line so that it also overlaps the left-hand side of the circle in the right-hand image. Making the same changes for the second pair means that E is the correct answer.

Pages 99–101: Paper 2, Section 4

1. B

The image rotates 90° clockwise at each step from left to right. Therefore, B is correct.

2. A

At each step, from left to right, the circle moves diagonally from the top left to the bottom right. The grey shading increases across the square at each step but alternates between the top left and the bottom right. Therefore, the correct answer is A.

3. E

At each step, from left to right, the semi-circle moves down the box and the rectangle moves up. Both shapes reduce in size as they do so. Therefore, the correct answer is E.

4. C

The hexagon rotates equally at each step from left to right. The answer is C because it shows the black-shaded segment in the correct position.

5. B

At each step, from left to right, the shapes in the top-left corner gradually increase in size. At the same time, an extra 'diameter' line is added to the circle and an extra side is added to the shape around it. The answer is B (as opposed to A) because the circle has the additional line in the correct place for the sequence.

6. E

At each step, from left to right, the arc rotates 90° clockwise around the box and the inner segment rotates 135° clockwise. Therefore, E is correct.

7. C

At each step, from left to right, a square is added at the top left corner of the box and any existing squares move from side to side and gradually towards the centre of the box. At each step, a circle is introduced from the bottom right corner of the box and any existing circles then move from side to side and gradually towards the centre of the box. Therefore, the correct answer is C.

8. C

The first, third and fifth boxes follow one sequence while the second and fourth boxes follow another. The answer is C because the opposite segment to that seen in the third box should be shaded black.

9. D

At each step, from left to right, the 'V' shapes move 90° anti-clockwise around the central black square. The two semi-circles move clockwise around the sides

of the box. The zig-zag line increases in length as it moves anti-clockwise around the box. Therefore, D is correct.

10. E

The pattern of the given boxes suggests that there is a vertical line of reflection through the third box, while the clockwise movement of the black circle suggests it should be in a central position on the bottom side of that box. Therefore, the only possible answers are D and E. The grid-patterned square (rather than the plain square) appears when the shapes are arranged in two lines of three, meaning that E is correct.

11. E

At each step, from left to right, a new circle is introduced at the centre of the box and any existing circles move first to the top right of the box, then to the top left, then to the bottom left and finally to the bottom right. The answer is E because the circle introduced at the centre of the third box must be one with a '+' style pattern, meaning that the circle with an 'x' style pattern moves to the top right.

12. E

At each step, from left to right, the diagonal lines reflect in a vertical line while the white circle moves diagonally from the top right to the bottom left. The black square moves clockwise around the corners and the triangle rotates 225° clockwise around the box. Therefore, E is correct.

Pages 102–104: Paper 2, Section 5

1. E

In the first row, the left-hand image rotates 90° anti-clockwise to produce the image on the right. Applying the same change to the second row means that E is the correct answer.

2. C

In the first row, the right-hand image is reflected in a vertical line to produce the image on the left. At the same time, the black inner shading on the circle moves to the outer part of the shape. Applying the same changes to the second row means that C is the correct answer.

3. E

In the first row, the left-hand image rotates 90° anti-clockwise to produce the image on the right. The circle changes from white to black as it does so. Applying the same changes to the second row means that E is the correct answer.

4. E

In the first two rows, from left to right, the black shape moves from the bottom right corner to the top left of the box and the arrow moves anti-clockwise to each corner of the box. Also, one of the two duplicated shapes stays fixed on the right side of the box while the other moves from the left to the right. Applying the same changes to the second row means that E is the correct answer.

5. D

In the first row, the shapes in the left-hand image are brought together with the introduction of a circle to create a

'face' in the right-hand image. As this happens, the component shapes alter: the triangle changes from white to black, the solid lines of the 'eyes' become dashed and the zig-zag line becomes 'wavy' as it forms the 'mouth'. Reversing these changes to the shapes in the second row, but bringing them together to form a 'face' again, means that D is correct.

6. E

In the first two rows, the square moves anti-clockwise to each successive corner of the box, increasing in size as it does so. So, in the middle box of the third row, a mid-sized square should be in the top right corner. The answer is E because it is the only option with the square in this position.

7. C

In the bottom two rows, one box has one shape, a second box has two shapes of the same kind and a third box has three shapes of the same kind. In the second row the black shape lies on top of the other shapes and in the third row the dotted shape lies on top. So in the first row, the missing box must contain two shapes of the same kind with the white one on top. Therefore, the answer is C.

8. D

In the first row, the triangle in the left-hand image is reflected in a vertical line and loses its shading to produce the right-hand image. The black-shaded square moves inside the triangle and the other two squares move to another corner of the box. One of these two squares remains white, while the other takes the shading of the original triangle. Applying these same changes to the shapes and shading in the second row means that D is the correct answer.

9. C

In the second column, the upper shape is reflected in a horizontal line to form the lower shape, but this does not apply to the pattern on the shape. The square remains on the upper part of the shape but reduces in size and the stripes remain on the lower part. Applying these changes in the first column means that C is the correct answer.

10. D

Looking at the outer boxes of the grid, there is a pattern of one, two, three and four circles and the answer options suggest that the empty box completes a similar pattern for the stripes. The stripes increase in number from the corner of the box nearest to the centre of the grid and an answer with three stripes is needed to complete the sequence of one, two, three, four. Therefore, the correct answer is D.

11. D

In the first and third rows, the arrow rotates 90° anti-clockwise from left to right and the accompanying shapes move from side to side with the upper shape increasing in size from left to right. This suggests that in the empty box of the second row, the arrow should be pointing to the bottom left with a large circle positioned at the top left. Therefore, the answer is D.

12. B

The number of shapes in each box increases by one from left to right through the columns, with one of these shapes shaded black and any additional shapes in white. Looking down the columns, the black shape appears to be in a consistent position (in an upper position in the first column, in a central position in the second column and in a lower position in the third column). You can therefore expect the empty box to have three shapes, one of which will be black and positioned at the bottom of the box. The empty box can also be expected to have a small triangle at the top left corner, in the same way that each row has one box with a circle at the top right. Therefore, the answer is B.

PRACTICE PAPER 3
Pages 106–108: Paper 3, Section 1

1. D

The two images on the left each show a smaller shape inside another figure of the same shape. Therefore, D is correct.

2. D

The two images on the left each show a larger shape and two circles. One of the circles is inside the shape and the other overlaps one side of the shape. In option A, one of the circles overlaps a corner rather than a side, therefore D is the only correct answer.

3. C

The two images on the left each show a circle divided into two components. Both component shapes have solid outlines and the smaller of the two has three stripes. Therefore, C is the correct answer.

4. E

The first image on the left shows three regular pentagons, one inside the other with the middle pentagon shaded black. The second image on the left shows three regular hexagons, again one inside the other with the middle hexagon shaded black. The correct answer is E because it shows three more regular polygons (squares) arranged in the same way.

5. C

The two images on the left each show a larger shape overlapped by two smaller figures of the same shape positioned opposite to each other. The black and white shading pattern is reversed between the two smaller shapes. C is the correct answer because it shows a trio of hexagons arranged in exactly the same way.

6. C

The two images on the left both have a vertical line of symmetry. Of the answer options, only C has a vertical line of symmetry and it is therefore correct.

7. A

The two images on the left both consist of a set of four figures of the same shape orientated in the same direction. One of the four shapes is placed to the top right of the largest shape, which makes A the correct answer rather than D.

8. B

The two images on the left are rotations of each other. B is the correct answer

because it is the only option that is a rotation of the images on the left.

9. A

The two images on the left both have eight identical 'tentacles'. A is the correct answer because it is the only option that has eight identical 'tentacles'.

10. A

The two images on the left are both four-sided shapes with straight sides. Option E has four sides but one is curved, so A is the correct answer.

11. D

The two images on the left both show a circle with a dashed outline surrounded by a circle with a solid outline. D is the correct answer because it is the only option with the same pattern of outlines.

12. A

The two images on the left both show circles divided into two segments, one larger than the other. The segments are marked by a line which touches the circumference but does not extend beyond it. A is the correct answer (rather than B or D) because it is the only option that shows a circle divided into two different-sized segments by a line which does not extend beyond the circumference.

Pages 109–111: Paper 3, Section 2

1. A

The upper letter is the code for the position of the shape and this is 'T' for the given image. The lower letter is the code for the shading pattern, so 'Y' is the code for stripes.

2. D

The upper letter is the code for the number of small stars and this is 'T' for the given image. The lower letter is the code for the shading pattern of the large star, so 'Z' is the code for black.

3. E

The upper letter is the code for the size of the triangle and this is 'R' for the given image. The lower letter is the code for the position of the black square, so 'W' is the code for the top right.

4. D

The upper letter is the code for the relative positions of the two shorter arrows (to the left or right of the central arrow) and this is 'Y' for the given image. The lower letter is the code for the direction of the longest arrow, so 'H' is the code for downwards.

5. A

The upper letter is the code for the direction of the arrow and this is 'T' for the given image. The lower letter is the code for the shading pattern, so 'K' is the code for dotted.

6. B

The upper letter is the code for the position of the circle (inside or outside the oval) and this is 'S' for the given image. The lower letter is the code for the orientation of the oval, so 'H' is the code for diagonal.

7. C

The upper letter is the code for the shading pattern and this is 'H' for the given image. The lower letter is the code

for the type of shape, so 'T' is the code for a rhombus.

8. D

The upper letter is the code for the shading pattern and this is 'K' for the given image. The lower letter is the code for the shape of the 'string', which is 'S' for the given image.

9. A

The upper letter is the code for the presence of a circle or a triangle and this is 'X' for the given image. The lower letter is the code for the style of the zig-zag line, which is 'K' for the given image.

10. A

The upper letter is the code for the proportion of shaded segments in the shape, so 'R' is the code for the given image in which half are shaded. The lower letter is the code for the shading pattern, so 'Y' is the code for a grid-style pattern.

11. C

The upper letter is the code for the shading of the shape with the rounded end, so 'Y' is the code for white in the given image. The lower letter is the code for the orientation of the shape and this is 'J' for the given image.

12. E

The upper letter is the code for the number of larger circles (none, one or two), so 'X' is the code for the given image, which has no larger circles. The lower letter is the code for the number of dots and this is 'K' for the given image, which has three.

Pages 112–114: Paper 3, Section 3

1. C

The answer is C because in all the other images the black square is positioned in a corner.

2. C

The answer is C because in each of the other options the figures used are exactly the same shape.

3. D

The answer is D because in all the other images the black dot is positioned in the smaller of the overlapping shapes.

4. E

The answer is E because in all the other images the arrow is pointing away from the black square.

5. D

The answer is D because the arrow in the central shape is pointing away from the straight-ended side unlike the other images.

6. C

The answer is C because all the other images have pentagons, rather than a quadrilateral, with dots at each corner.

7. B

The answer is B because in all the other images the striped shading in the square and triangles runs in the same direction. B is the only image which has both vertical and horizontal striped shading.

8. B

The answer is B because in all the other images the two angles are marked by one curved arc in combination with one 'squared' arc. B is the only image in which the angles are marked by two 'squared' arcs.

9. **D**

   The answer is D because in all the other images the opposite-facing circular shapes have a matching pattern. In option D, one of the pairs of circular shapes does not have a matching pattern.

10. **D**

   The answer is D because in all the other images the outer black circle is positioned on the other side of the figure, relative to the white circle.

11. **C**

   The answer is C because in all the other images the black arcs on the circles on the upper triangle are aligned towards the black arcs that are in the corners of the lower triangle. In option C, two of the black arcs on the upper triangle are not aligned to the black arcs on the lower triangle.

12. **A**

   The answer is A because the sequence of the shaded semi-circles is different to that used in the other images.

Pages 115–117: Paper 3, Section 4

1. **B**

   When viewed from above, the figure shows three cubes in the front row, three cubes in the middle row and one cube in the back row, aligned with the right-hand side of the first two rows.

2. **E**

   When viewed from above, the figure shows two cubes in the front row, two cubes in the middle row and one cube in the back row. The middle row has cubes that are aligned to the right-hand side of the front row, sticking out by one place, and the back row is central.

3. **B**

   When viewed from above, the figure shows two cubes in each of the front and second rows, and one cube in each of the third and fourth rows. The third and fourth rows are aligned to the right-hand side of the front rows.

4. **B**

   When viewed from above, the figure has three cubes in the front row, three cubes in the middle row (aligned two to the left-hand side of the front row, one overhanging, and one to the right-hand side, attached by the corner) and one cube in the back row.

5. **C**

   When viewed from above, the figure has five cubes in a single row.

6. **A**

   When viewed from above, the figure has two cubes in the front row, three cubes in the middle row and one cube in the back row. The front row is aligned to the left-hand side of the middle row, and the back row is aligned to the right-hand side of the middle row.

7. **D**

   When viewed from above, the figure has three cubes in the front row, separated into a single cube on the left-hand side and two cubes on the right-hand side. It has four cubes in the back row.

8. **D**

   When viewed from above, the figure has four cubes in the front row, three cubes in the middle row and three cubes in the back row. The middle and back rows are aligned with the right-hand side of the front row.

9. **B**

   When viewed from above, the figure has four cubes in the front row, three cubes in the second row and one cube in the third row. You can eliminate option D as there is clearly no fourth cube in the second row on the left-hand side.

10. **B**

   When viewed from above, the figure has four cubes in the front row and three cubes in the back row. The back row has two cubes to the left-hand side of the front row, overhanging by one cube, and one cube to the right-hand side.

11. **A**

   When viewed from above, the figure has one cube in the front row, four cubes in the second row, one cube in the third row and one cube in the fourth row. The front row is aligned with the second cube from the left of the second row and the third and fourth rows are aligned with the right-hand side of the second row.

12. **C**

   When viewed from above, the figure has three cubes in the front row and two cubes in the back row, aligned with the left-hand side and centre of the front row.

Pages 118–120: Paper 3, Section 5

1. **C**

   In the first pair, the left-hand image rotates 45° and the sides join together to produce the right-hand image. Making the same change for the second pair means that C is the correct answer.

2. **E**

   In the first pair, the larger triangle (but not the inner triangle) and the patterned triangles reflect in a vertical line to produce the right-hand image. At the same time, the patterned triangles also swap places. Making the same changes for the second pair means that E is the correct answer.

3. **C**

   In the first pair, a black triangle is super-imposed over the white triangle to produce the right-hand image. The black triangle is orientated in the opposite direction to the white triangle. Making the same changes for the second pair means that C is the correct answer.

4. **E**

   In the first pair, the two ovals enlarge and surround the 'S' shape (which reduces in size) to produce the right-hand image. The shapes remain orientated in the same direction. Making the same changes for the second pair means that E is the correct answer.

5. **C**

   In the first pair, the two squares inside the circle become two circles inside a square in the right-hand image. At the same time, the outline used for a circle changes from dashed to a heavy, solid style. In the second

pair, you can expect the changes to occur in reverse, since the starting image consists of a large triangle with a solid outline enclosing two squares with heavy, solid outlines. Therefore, C is the correct answer.

6. **D**

   In the first pair, the left-hand image rotates 90° clockwise to produce the right-hand image. Making the same change for the second pair means that D is the correct answer.

7. **A**

   In the first pair, a circle split into thirds changes to a circle divided into sixths. The shading that was used in the lower third of the initial circle fills three alternate segments of the second circle, while the black square that was in the right-hand third of the initial circle occupies two of the left-hand segments in the second circle. Making the same pattern changes to the same segments for the second pair means that A is the correct answer.

8. **B**

   In the first pair, the left-hand image rotates 90° clockwise to produce the right-hand image. The square is duplicated so that it 'slots' into either side of the larger shape and the shapes swap shading. Making the same changes for the second pair means that B is the correct answer.

9. **E**

   In the first pair, the left-hand image rotates 90° anti-clockwise to produce the right-hand image. The two smaller shapes are also reflected to opposite sides of the larger shape. Making these changes for the second pair means that E is the correct answer.

10. **A**

   In the first pair, the shapes in the left-hand image change size and position to produce the right-hand image. The outer hexagon reduces in size and encloses the circle, which moves from the top left to the centre of the image. The square becomes the largest, outer shape and it rotates 45° as it does so. Making the same changes for the second pair means that A is the correct answer.

11. **B**

   In the first pair, the two shapes in the left-hand image swap sizes and shading to produce the right-hand image. At the same time, the smaller (black-shaded) of the two shapes moves from the side to the centre of the other shape. Making the same changes for the second pair means that B is the correct answer.

12. **E**

   In the first pair, the left-hand image rotates 180° and changes from black to white to produce the right-hand image. Making these changes in reverse for the second pair means that E is the correct answer.

PRACTICE PAPER 4
Pages 122–124: Paper 4, Section 1

1. **D**

   There are two alternating sequences – one for the first, third and fifth boxes and one for the second and fourth boxes. The shapes swap sides in the first and third boxes, suggesting that the fifth box will see them return to their original positions. Therefore, D is correct.

2. **B**

There are two alternating sequences – one for the first, third and fifth boxes and one for the second and fourth boxes. Between the first and the third box, the circle moves two squares anti-clockwise and the striped pattern moves two squares clockwise and rotates 90°. The black square and the cross remain in the same position. Therefore, the correct answer is B.

3. **B**

At each step, from left to right, the arrow rotates 45° clockwise and the small square and small circle move clockwise around the corners of the box, alternating between black and white shading as they do so. Therefore, the correct answer is B.

4. **A**

At each step, from left to right, the black rectangle moves from one side of the box to the other, while the white rectangle moves clockwise around the sides of the box. In the fourth box, the two rectangles will occupy the same position. The triangle moves up and down the middle of the box in steps. Therefore, the correct answer is A.

5. **A**

At each step, from right to left, there are two fewer stripes and the grey box reduces in size and moves anti-clockwise around the corners of the box. The diagonal line alternates its position, leaving only A and D as the possible answers, but A is correct because the stripes and the square lie on either side of the line rather than on the same side.

6. **B**

At each step, from left to right, the black circle moves clockwise around the sides of the box while the 'tube' rotates 60° clockwise. So the 'tube' will be in an upright position in the fourth box, with the black circle positioned at the bottom of the box. Therefore, the correct answer is B.

7. **E**

At each step, from left to right, the black circles increase in number by one and the point from which they start moves one place clockwise around the edge of the box. At the same time, the rectangle moves down the centre of the box and the direction of its shading alternates. Therefore, the correct answer is E.

8. **E**

At each step, from left to right, the central circle alternates between black and white, while two 'petals' are lost. As shown by the third and fourth boxes, the petals are lost in an anti-clockwise direction from the top, hence the correct answer is E rather than D.

9. **D**

At each step, from left to right, an extra circle is added inside a shape. The shape's number of sides reduces by one at each

step, so the missing box will consist of a quadrilateral enclosing four circles. Therefore, the correct answer is D.

10. **C**

At each step, from left to right, the striped pattern moves in a clockwise direction around the corner triangles of the box while the white circle moves in an anti-clockwise direction. The white triangle and black shading also move around the inner triangles in opposite directions to each other. Therefore, the correct answer is C.

11. **D**

At each step, from left to right, the small white square moves from the bottom left corner to the top left corner and back again. The curved shape moves anti-clockwise around the corners of the box, while the diagonal line moves clockwise around the corners. The three black circles stay in fixed positions. Therefore, the correct answer is D.

12. **B**

At each step, from left to right, the shaded segments move one place in an anti-clockwise direction, while the black circle moves two segments in an anti-clockwise direction. Therefore, the correct answer is B.

Pages 125–127: Paper 4, Section 2

1. **C**

From left to right in the first and third rows, the larger shape rotates 90° anti-clockwise as it moves in an anti-clockwise direction around the sides of the box. The shading moves one column to the left down each row. The smaller shapes remain in a fixed position in each column. Applying the same changes to the second row means that C is the correct answer.

2. **C**

In the first row, the shading reverses within the figure from the left column to the right. Applying the same change to the second row means that C is the correct answer.

3. **B**

In the second and third rows, the larger shape rotates 90° clockwise as it moves clockwise around the sides of the box and increases in number by one in each column from left to right. The smaller shape moves clockwise by half the length of a side in each column. Applying the same changes to the first row means that B is the correct answer.

4. **B**

In the first row, the shape is reflected in a vertical line and any solid outlines become dashed (and vice-versa) in the next column. Applying the same changes to the second row means that B is the correct answer.

5. **C**

In the first and second rows, there is one box with two shapes, another box with four shapes and a third box with six shapes. In each box, half of the shapes are white and half are black. The third row already has boxes of two and of six squares, so the empty box will have four

squares with two shaded black and two white. Therefore, C is the correct answer.

6. **E**

In the first two columns, the shapes rotate 90° clockwise and one shape is shaded black, one white and one dotted. A dotted shape is needed in the empty box of the third column and it should be rotated 90° clockwise from the position in the top box. Therefore, E is the correct answer.

7. **E**

In the bottom row, the small square can be expected to move to the opposite bottom corner and change its cross pattern in the same way as the circle does in the top corners of the top row. This means only B and E are possible answers. E is correct because the shading on the diagonal image needs to reverse in the same way as it does in the top row.

8. **B**

From the top row downwards, the shapes move one column to the right and reduce in size, but do not rotate. Therefore, B is the correct answer.

9. **A**

In the second row, from left to right, the dotted pattern of the oval moves to the opposite quarter and the small, white oval moves up to take its place in the top left. In the first row, the striped rectangle and the small, black rectangle make these same movements, leaving A and C as the only possible options. The answer is A because the three triangles on the left of the box are correctly orientated based on the semi-circles in the second row.

10. **D**

In each of the given boxes, the circle rotates 90° clockwise as it moves clockwise around the corners of the box from left to right. The other shaded (or patterned) shape interchanges between opposite corners from left to right across the columns. The answer is D because the half-shaded circle and the triangle with the dot are in the correct corners and the circle has been correctly rotated.

11. **C**

The two dotted shields in the second column follow the movement and the shading change that occurs to the two white triangles (which move down the box and change to black) in the first column. The white single shield reverses its direction, enlarges and changes shading in the same way as the single black triangle in the top row of the first column. Therefore, the answer is C.

12. **A**

The first and third rows indicate that the middle column should be occupied by a large black shape and a separate, smaller white shape. Therefore, the answer is A.

Pages 128–130: Paper 4, Section 3

1. **B**

The three single-headed arrows on the left all pass through the centre of the circle. The answer is B because it is the only option where a single-headed arrow passes through the centre.

2. D

The three images on the left all show a shape that contains only black circles. The answer is D because it is the only option with a black circle inside the shape.

3. E

The three images on the left all show a 'snowman' with a white hat and three 'buttons'. The three buttons are polygons. The answer is E because the three buttons are triangles (i.e. polygons) and the hat is correctly sized and shaded.

4. A

The three images on the left all show 'lines' on a 'double page'. The 'lines' are curved or straight to match the shape of the edge of the page. The answer is A because it is the only option with matching lines and page shape.

5. E

The three images on the left all have an odd number of sides (3, 5 and 9). The answer is E because it also has an odd number of sides (7), whereas the other options have an even number of sides.

6. B

The three images on the left all show an arrow wrapped around a 'stand' that has perpendicular lines. B and C are therefore the only possible options but the answer is B because the horizontal line in C is much thicker than the lines used on the left.

7. D

The three images on the left all show a shape touching either the top or the bottom of a circle at one point only. The answer is D (rather than A or C) because the shape is correctly positioned at the top of the circle.

8. A

The three images on the left all show a 'crown' with five 'jewels' on the tips. The answer is A because it is the only option with five 'jewels'.

9. D

The three images on the left show concentric shapes that enlarge from a point on the edge of the smallest figure. The answer is D because it is the only option where the enlargement takes place from the edge of the original figure.

10. E

The three shapes on the left are all four-sided figures. Therefore, the only possible options are C and E but the answer is E because, like the images on the left, it doesn't have any internal lines.

11. B

The three images on the left show figures that are each comprised of 11 of one type of shape only. The answer is B because it is the only option that is comprised of 11 shapes of the same kind.

12. D

The three images on the left show a single arrowhead spiralling outwards with acute and right-angle turns. Option A has curved turns and options B and E have two arrowheads, so the only possible answer is D.

Pages 131–134: Paper 4, Section 4

1. B

The codes are: V = curved, inverted L-shape; W = straight-edged, inverted L-shape; I = one stripe; P = two stripes; Z = three stripes.

2. E

The codes are: B = bottom left-hand square has a diagonal stripe going from bottom left to top right; D = bottom left-hand square has a diagonal stripe going from top left to bottom right; Y = bottom left-hand square has a vertical stripe; N = top right-hand square is shaded grey; P = top right-hand square has horizontal striped shading; M = top right-hand square has vertical striped shading.

3. D

The codes are: S = diagonal striped shading going from bottom left to top right; R = diagonal striped shading going from top left to bottom right; Q = black dot; W = white dot; E = isosceles triangle; F = equilateral triangle; G = scalene triangle.

4. E

The codes are: Q = black triangle on left-hand side of striped triangle; E = black triangle on right-hand side of striped triangle; V = black-shaded quadrilateral at bottom right-hand side of figure; D = bold vertical stripe in quadrilateral at bottom right-hand side of figure; P = dotted shading in quadrilateral at bottom right-hand side of figure; F = bold cross in quadrilateral at bottom right-hand side of figure.

5. B

The codes are: F = circles arranged in diagonal line; O = circles offset in a vertical line; A = circles arranged in horizontal line; Y = one circle shaded black; J = three circles shaded black; P = two circles shaded black.

6. B

The codes are: E = black triangle; F = white triangle; A = triangle to far left of rectangle; B = triangle to middle left of rectangle; C = triangle to middle right of rectangle; D = triangle to far right of rectangle; G = one dot; H = two dots.

7. E

The codes are: M = alternate diagonal lines of the octagon are bold; T = alternate horizontal and vertical lines of the octagon are bold; B = no bold lines on the octagon; Q = shaded area in bottom right-hand side of the octagon; G = shaded area in top left-hand side of the octagon; P = vertical striped shading; V = diagonal striped shading.

8. A

The codes are: A = two lines dividing the circle; B = one line dividing the circle; C = three lines dividing the circle; D = four lines dividing the circle; Z = dividing lines on left-hand side of the circle; Y = dividing lines at the top of the circle; X = dividing lines at the bottom of the circle.

9. A

The codes are: F = black dot; G = no black dot; H = rectangle on right-hand side of square; I = rectangle on left-hand side of square; J = rectangle at bottom of square; K = square divided into two white parts; L = square divided into three white parts; M = square divided into four white parts; N = square divided into five white parts.

10. C

The codes are: R = small triangle; Z = small square; Q = black and white rectangles; O = only black rectangle; V = black rectangle on right-hand side of semi-circle; Y = black rectangle on left-hand side of semi-circle.

11. C

The codes are: G = 'V' lines point upwards; F = 'V' lines point downwards; T = black square; P = white square; O = diagonal striped square running from bottom left to top right; Z = diagonal striped square running from top left to bottom right; A = circles at either end of the horizontal line; B = short straight lines at either end of the horizontal line; N = twirled ends of the horizontal line.

12. E

The codes are: A = black dot in upper right-hand corner; H = white dot in upper right-hand corner; C = brickwork made up of two blocks in the top row, three in the bottom row; D = brickwork made up of three blocks in the top row, two in the bottom row; E = brickwork made up of three blocks in the top row, three in the bottom row; N = diagonal line has flat ends; V = diagonal line has fine arrowheads at either end; W = diagonal line has triangular arrowheads at either end; F = diagonal line has turned flat ends.

Pages 135–137: Paper 4, Section 5

1. A

The trapezium appears in option A.

2. E

The parallelogram appears in option E.

3. C

The irregular pentagon appears in option C.

4. E

The arrowhead appears in option E.

5. A

The arrowhead appears in option A.

6. B

The isosceles triangle appears in option B.

7. B

The scalene triangle appears in option B.

8. B

The irregular hexagon appears in option B.

9. E

The trapezium appears in option E.

10. A

The quadrilateral appears in option A.

11. B

The rectangle with two curved corners appears in option B.

12. B

The irregular octagon appears in option B.

Progress Charts

Track your progress by shading in your score at each attempt.

Practice Papers

	Score	Date:	Attempt 1	Paper 1: Section 1
/12	Score	Date:	Attempt 2	
/12	Score	Date:	Attempt 1	Paper 1: Section 2
/12	Score	Date:	Attempt 2	
/12	Score	Date:	Attempt 1	Paper 1: Section 3
/12	Score	Date:	Attempt 2	
/12	Score	Date:	Attempt 1	Paper 1: Section 4
/12	Score	Date:	Attempt 2	
/12	Score	Date:	Attempt 1	Paper 1: Section 5
/12	Score	Date:	Attempt 2	
/12	Score	Date:	Attempt 1	Paper 2: Section 1
/12	Score	Date:	Attempt 2	
/12	Score	Date:	Attempt 1	Paper 2: Section 2
/12	Score	Date:	Attempt 2	
/12	Score	Date:	Attempt 1	Paper 2: Section 3
/12	Score	Date:	Attempt 2	
/12	Score	Date:	Attempt 1	Paper 2: Section 4
/12	Score	Date:	Attempt 2	
/12	Score	Date:	Attempt 1	Paper 2: Section 5
/12	Score	Date:	Attempt 2	
/12	Score	Date:	Attempt 1	Paper 3: Section 1
/12	Score	Date:	Attempt 2	
/12	Score	Date:	Attempt 1	Paper 3: Section 2
/12	Score	Date:	Attempt 2	
/12	Score	Date:	Attempt 1	Paper 3: Section 3
/12	Score	Date:	Attempt 2	
/12	Score	Date:	Attempt 1	Paper 3: Section 4
/12	Score	Date:	Attempt 2	
/12	Score	Date:	Attempt 1	Paper 3: Section 5
/12	Score	Date:	Attempt 2	
/12	Score	Date:	Attempt 1	Paper 4: Section 1
/12	Score	Date:	Attempt 2	
/12	Score	Date:	Attempt 1	Paper 4: Section 2
/12	Score	Date:	Attempt 2	
/12	Score	Date:	Attempt 1	Paper 4: Section 3
/12	Score	Date:	Attempt 2	
/12	Score	Date:	Attempt 1	Paper 4: Section 4
/12	Score	Date:	Attempt 2	
/12	Score	Date:	Attempt 1	Paper 4: Section 5
/12	Score	Date:	Attempt 2	

Practice Tests

	Score	Date:	Attempt 1	Practice Test 1:
/11	Score	Date:	Attempt 2	Making Connections
/14	Score	Date:	Attempt 1	Practice Test 2:
/14	Score	Date:	Attempt 2	Breaking Codes
/14	Score	Date:	Attempt 1	Practice Test 3:
/14	Score	Date:	Attempt 2	Finding Relationships
/8	Score	Date:	Attempt 1	Practice Test 4:
/8	Score	Date:	Attempt 2	Spotting Patterns
/14	Score	Date:	Attempt 1	Practice Test 5:
/14	Score	Date:	Attempt 2	Completing Sequences
/10	Score	Date:	Attempt 1	Practice Test 6:
/10	Score	Date:	Attempt 2	Spatial Reasoning
/46	Score	Date:	Attempt 1	Practice Test 7:
/46	Score	Date:	Attempt 2	Mixed Practice

Pupil's Name		Date of Test
School Name		

Please mark like this ⊢.

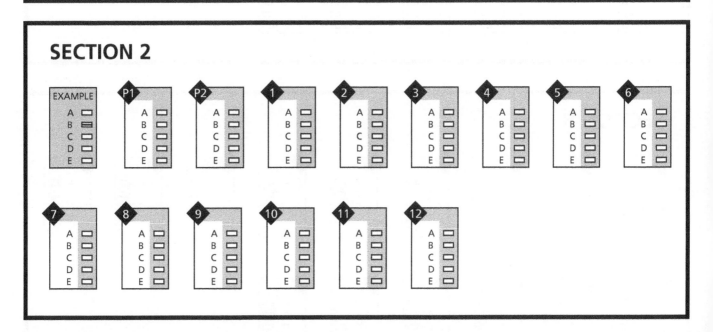

SECTION 1

EXAMPLE P1 P2 1 2 3 4 5 6 7 8 9 10 11 12
A B C D E

SECTION 2

EXAMPLE P1 P2 1 2 3 4 5 6 7 8 9 10 11 12
A B C D E

SECTION 3

SECTION 4

SECTION 5

        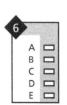

  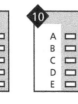  

Pupil's Name		Date of Test

School Name

PUPIL NUMBER

[0]	[0]	[0]	[0]	[0]	[0]
[1]	[1]	[1]	[1]	[1]	[1]
[2]	[2]	[2]	[2]	[2]	[2]
[3]	[3]	[3]	[3]	[3]	[3]
[4]	[4]	[4]	[4]	[4]	[4]
[5]	[5]	[5]	[5]	[5]	[5]
[6]	[6]	[6]	[6]	[6]	[6]
[7]	[7]	[7]	[7]	[7]	[7]
[8]	[8]	[8]	[8]	[8]	[8]
[9]	[9]	[9]	[9]	[9]	[9]

SCHOOL NUMBER

[0]	[0]	[0]	[0]	[0]	[0]	[0]
[1]	[1]	[1]	[1]	[1]	[1]	[1]
[2]	[2]	[2]	[2]	[2]	[2]	[2]
[3]	[3]	[3]	[3]	[3]	[3]	[3]
[4]	[4]	[4]	[4]	[4]	[4]	[4]
[5]	[5]	[5]	[5]	[5]	[5]	[5]
[6]	[6]	[6]	[6]	[6]	[6]	[6]
[7]	[7]	[7]	[7]	[7]	[7]	[7]
[8]	[8]	[8]	[8]	[8]	[8]	[8]
[9]	[9]	[9]	[9]	[9]	[9]	[9]

Please mark like this ⊢.

DATE OF BIRTH

Day	Month	Year
[0] [0]	January ▢	2007 ▢
[1] [1]	February ▢	2008 ▢
[2] [2]	March ▢	2009 ▢
[3] [3]	April ▢	2010 ▢
[4]	May ▢	2011 ▢
[5]	June ▢	2012 ▢
[6]	July ▢	2013 ▢
[7]	August ▢	2014 ▢
[8]	September ▢	2015 ▢
[9]	October ▢	2016 ▢
	November ▢	2017 ▢
	December ▢	2018 ▢

SECTION 1

     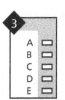 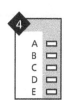

  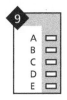   

SECTION 2

      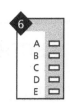

    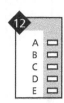

SECTION 3

SECTION 4

    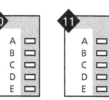

SECTION 5

   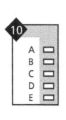  

NON-VERBAL REASONING PRACTICE PAPER 3

NVR 3

Pupil's Name

School Name

Date of Test

DATE OF BIRTH

Day	Month	Year
[0] [0]	January	2007
[1] [1]	February	2008
[2] [2]	March	2009
[3] [3]	April	2010
[4]	May	2011
[5]	June	2012
[6]	July	2013
[7]	August	2014
[8]	September	2015
[9]	October	2016
	November	2017
	December	2018

PUPIL NUMBER

[0] [0] [0] [0] [0] [0]
[1] [1] [1] [1] [1] [1]
[2] [2] [2] [2] [2] [2]
[3] [3] [3] [3] [3] [3]
[4] [4] [4] [4] [4] [4]
[5] [5] [5] [5] [5] [5]
[6] [6] [6] [6] [6] [6]
[7] [7] [7] [7] [7] [7]
[8] [8] [8] [8] [8] [8]
[9] [9] [9] [9] [9] [9]

SCHOOL NUMBER

[0] [0] [0] [0] [0] [0] [0]
[1] [1] [1] [1] [1] [1] [1]
[2] [2] [2] [2] [2] [2] [2]
[3] [3] [3] [3] [3] [3] [3]
[4] [4] [4] [4] [4] [4] [4]
[5] [5] [5] [5] [5] [5] [5]
[6] [6] [6] [6] [6] [6] [6]
[7] [7] [7] [7] [7] [7] [7]
[8] [8] [8] [8] [8] [8] [8]
[9] [9] [9] [9] [9] [9] [9]

Please mark like this ⊢.

SECTION 1

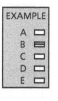   

SECTION 2

SECTION 3

  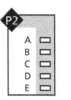 

SECTION 4

      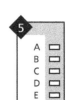 

SECTION 5

Pupil's Name		Date of Test
School Name		

PUPIL NUMBER

[0]	[0]	[0]	[0]	[0]	[0]
[1]	[1]	[1]	[1]	[1]	[1]
[2]	[2]	[2]	[2]	[2]	[2]
[3]	[3]	[3]	[3]	[3]	[3]
[4]	[4]	[4]	[4]	[4]	[4]
[5]	[5]	[5]	[5]	[5]	[5]
[6]	[6]	[6]	[6]	[6]	[6]
[7]	[7]	[7]	[7]	[7]	[7]
[8]	[8]	[8]	[8]	[8]	[8]
[9]	[9]	[9]	[9]	[9]	[9]

SCHOOL NUMBER

[0]	[0]	[0]	[0]	[0]	[0]	[0]
[1]	[1]	[1]	[1]	[1]	[1]	[1]
[2]	[2]	[2]	[2]	[2]	[2]	[2]
[3]	[3]	[3]	[3]	[3]	[3]	[3]
[4]	[4]	[4]	[4]	[4]	[4]	[4]
[5]	[5]	[5]	[5]	[5]	[5]	[5]
[6]	[6]	[6]	[6]	[6]	[6]	[6]
[7]	[7]	[7]	[7]	[7]	[7]	[7]
[8]	[8]	[8]	[8]	[8]	[8]	[8]
[9]	[9]	[9]	[9]	[9]	[9]	[9]

DATE OF BIRTH

Day		Month		Year	
[0]	[0]	January ▭		2007 ▭	
[1]	[1]	February ▭		2008 ▭	
[2]	[2]	March ▭		2009 ▭	
[3]	[3]	April ▭		2010 ▭	
	[4]	May ▭		2011 ▭	
	[5]	June ▭		2012 ▭	
	[6]	July ▭		2013 ▭	
	[7]	August ▭		2014 ▭	
	[8]	September ▭		2015 ▭	
	[9]	October ▭		2016 ▭	
		November ▭		2017 ▭	
		December ▭		2018 ▭	

Please mark like this ⊢.

SECTION 1

SECTION 2

     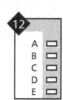

SECTION 3

  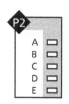 

 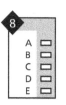   

SECTION 4

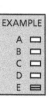 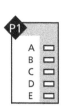     

SECTION 5

 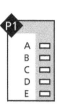   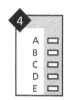